TEACH YOURSELF...
CORELDRAW

BY MAXINE IRITZ

MIS:
PRESS

A Subsidiary of
Henry Holt and Co., Inc.

ISBN 1-55828-233-5

First Edition—1992

Printed in the United States of America

10 9 8 7 6 5 4 3 2 1

MIS:Press books are available at special discounts for bulk purchases for sales promotions, premiums, fund-raising, or educational use. Special editions or book excerpts can also be created to specification.

For details contact: Special Sales Director
MIS:Press
a subsidiary of Henry Holt and Company, Inc.
115 West 18th Street
New York, NY 10011

Development Editor: Kathleen Joyce

Editing and layout: Dawn Erdos

DEDICATION

To the folks at Asymtek.

TABLE OF CONTENTS

CHAPTER 13:
CORELPHOTO-PAINT..223

CHAPTER 18:
CHARTING WITH CORELCHART 307

INTRODUCTION

CorelDRAW is one of the most powerful, versatile, and comprehensive graphics programs on the market today. With it, you can create exciting powerful graphics, incorporate text and graphics from other programs, and provide all types of graphic data to other programs, such as word processors or desktop publishers. This chapter covers:

▼ What is CorelDRAW?
▼ Microsoft Windows.
▼ Mousing Around.
▼ Installing CorelDRAW.
▼ Using Help.
▼ How To Use This Book.

1

WHAT IS CORELDRAW?

Actually, the new CorelDRAW, version 3.0, consists of six different applications, designed to give you a "studio in a box."

- ▼ **CorelDRAW**, the heart of the system, is the basic illustration program. With it, you can create graphics and text, manage your files, and import and export files between CorelDRAW and other software.

- ▼ **CorelPHOTO-PAINT** is a color image editing and paint program. It gives you a full range of painting and retouching tools and lets you create new bitmapped images and spruce up existing ones.

- ▼ **CorelCHART** develops and displays charts of all types. This powerful data manager lets you enter data and calculate results and accepts spreadsheet data from Lotus 1-2-3 and Microsoft Excel.

- ▼ **CorelSHOW** creates presentations, allowing you to import artwork (such as Corel charts) from any Windows application. You can use both animated and still files, and add transitional effects between images to create on-screen slideshows.

- ▼ **CorelTRACE** traces almost any kind of bitmapped artwork, including scanned data.

- ▼ **Mosaic** helps you to find and manage your files, giving you graphical thumbnail sketches, or previews, of your data, and to perform some batch processing such as printing.

The very features that make CorelDRAW so powerful also make it somewhat difficult to learn without help. The purpose of this book is to help you get started with as little pain and as much fun as possible.

NOTE   Do yourself a favor and watch the video that came with your software. It's a great way to get the big picture quickly and painlessly.

This book is organized very simply. It begins by going over the basics, such as installing CorelDRAW and navigating your way around the screen, both via mouse and keyboard. It includes a quick overview of the menus and the toolbox options, to give you a summary of the functions you can perform. Alternate methods and shortcuts are also covered, as well as several features designed to make your life with CorelDRAW a lot easier.

▼ Chapter 1 introduces CorelDRAW, describes some of the basic elements of Microsoft Windows, and explains how to install the CorelDRAW programs.

▼ Chapter 2 describes how to access the CorelDRAW applications and describes the basic elements of the CorelDRAW screen.

▼ Chapter 3 teaches you how to set preferences and how to draw rectangles and ellipses.

▼ Chapter 4 covers how to draw lines and curves and how to use the Pick tool and the Transform menu to modify the shapes you have drawn.

▼ Chapter 5 helps you make your graphics more interesting by using fills and outlines.

▼ Chapter 6 describes how to shape lines, curves, rectangles, and ellipses.

▼ Chapter 7 teaches you how to add text and symbols to your graphics and how to manipulate and shape these objects.

▼ Chapter 8 covers the options in the File menu.

▼ Chapter 9 demonstrates how to manipulate objects using the Arrange menu.

▼ Chapter 10 shows you how to apply envelopes, perspective, blends, and extrusion for special effects.

▼ Chapter 11 explains how to use Mosaic to manage your files.

▼ Chapter 12 describes how to refine scanned images with CorelTRACE.

▼ Chapter 13 demonstrates the CorelPHOTO-PAINT drawing tools.

▼ Chapter 14 describes the CorelPHOTO-PAINT display and selection tools.

▼ Chapter 15 covers the CorelPHOTO-PAINT retouching tools.

▼ Chapter 16 gives you an overview of CorelCHART.

▼ Chapter 17 teaches you how to enter and import data into CorelCHART.

▼ Chapter 19 explains how to create a CorelSHOW presentation.

Before we get into CorelDRAW, however, let's back up and discuss some preliminaries—Microsoft Windows (which must be on your computer before you can even install CorelDRAW), the installation process, and how to use CorelDRAW Help.

MICROSOFT WINDOWS

Microsoft Windows is a graphical operating system that allows you to move easily between different applications, and even pass data between applications. If you haven't yet installed Windows on your system, do so now. You cannot install or use CorelDRAW without it.

 Although you can run CorelDRAW with Windows 3.0, you need to install Windows 3.1 to take advantage of all of its features. CorelCHART requires Windows 3.1 to run, and certain features of CorelSHOW also require Windows 3.1. An installation of CorelDRAW 3.0 using Windows 3.0 may take hours—twenty-eight is the record to date!

Although you do not need to be a Windows expert to use CorelDRAW, it's a good idea to learn some of the basics first. Try running the Windows Tutorial, or refer to the *Getting Started with Microsoft Windows* manual to give you an overview of Windows.

WINDOWS BASICS

To help you out a bit, we'll give you a brief look at the Windows screen, so that you can become acquainted with some pertinent terminology. Figure 1.1 shows a basic Microsoft Windows screen.

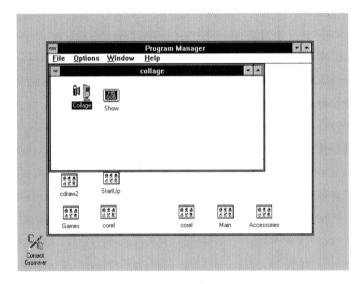

Figure 1.1 *The Microsoft Windows screen.*

Let's look at the various elements on the screen.

▼ **Desktop.** The entire screen area.

▼ **Window.** The part of the screen that shows an application or a group.

▼ **Icon.** A pictorial representation or symbol for an application or group.

▼ **Title Bar.** The area containing the names of an application or group.

▼ **Application.** A program that performs a particular function, such as word processing, graphics, or charting, for example, CorelCHART.

▼ **Group.** A collection of applications, such as CorelDRAW or Games.

▼ **Minimize button.** Reduces the application window to an icon.

▼ **Maximize button.** Enlarges the application window to fill the entire screen.

If you maximize a window, the Maximize button is replaced by a Restore button, represented by a double-headed arrow. This lets you return the window to its previous size.

▼ **Scroll bars.** Move "hidden" parts of a document into view.

▼ **Control menu box.** Allows you to access the control menu, shown in Figure 1.2.

The Control menu contains the following options:

♦ **Restore** returns the window to its previous size.

♦ **Move** lets you use the Arrow keys to move the window.

♦ **Size** lets you use the Arrow keys to resize the window.

♦ **Minimize** reduces the window to an icon.

♦ **Maximize** enlarges the window to fill the entire screen.

♦ **Close** closes the window or dialog box.

♦ **Switch To** allows you to move to another application without closing the current one.

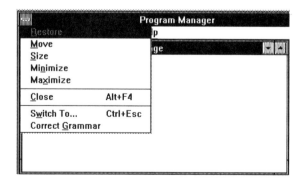

Figure 1.2 *The Windows Control menu.*

MOUSING AROUND

Although you can use the keyboard to perform most Windows functions, you'll find that using your mouse is the most efficient way to work in Windows. Let's cover some basic terms.

- ▼ **Point.** Move the mouse until the screen pointer rests on the item you want.
- ▼ **Click.** Quickly press and release the mouse button.
- ▼ **Double-click.** Quickly press and release the mouse button twice.
- ▼ **Drag** or **click and drag.** Hold down the mouse button while you move the mouse.

INSTALLING CORELDRAW

Installing CorelDRAW 3.0 is a simple but lengthy process. Reserve at least half an hour to install this program—you may want to use your waiting time to thumb through this book and give yourself a quick view of what's in store.

Before you begin, make sure that you're prepared. You'll need:

- ▼ A 386- or 486-type computer.
- ▼ Windows 3.1.
- ▼ 2 MB of memory (at the beginning of the installation process, CorelDRAW verifies that there is enough memory available before continuing).
- ▼ A graphic monitor.
- ▼ A mouse or other pointing device.

To begin the installation, open the Windows Program Manager, and select **Run** from the File menu. In the Command Line field of the dialog box, type *A:SETUP* (or *B:SETUP* if you're running the installation from the B: disk drive), then click on **OK**.

Simply follow along with the installation procedure. Setup lets you know when it needs information from you. You may choose to only install portions of the complete package, or accept the default installation.

USING HELP

All of the CorelDRAW 3.0 applications have a Help menu, which you can access from the Main menu. Click on **Help** or press **F1** to access Help.

The easiest way to use Help is to click on the **Index** option, then browse through the list of topics for which help is available. To get help for one of the items in the index, double-click on the item, and the information for that topic is displayed on the screen.

If you know exactly what you need help for, select **Search**, and type a keyword or phrase. Help displays the available information.

HOW TO USE THIS BOOK

To use this book most effectively, follow along on your computer. Learning computer programs, particularly graphics, is a hands-on task. So, book in hand, mouse poised to run, fingers on the keyboard, teach yourself CorelDRAW.

AN OVERVIEW OF CORELDRAW 3.0

This chapter covers:

▼ Starting CorelDRAW.

▼ The CorelDRAW screen.

9

STARTING CORELDRAW

To begin CorelDRAW, type *win* at the DOS prompt, then double-click on the Corel group icon. The Corel Graphics window, shown in Figure 2.1, is displayed.

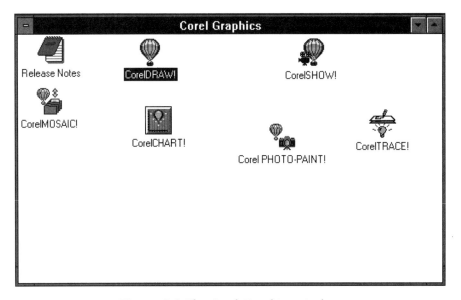

Figure 2.1 *The Corel Graphics window.*

Notice that there are six icons in this window, representing different CorelDRAW 3.0 applications. Double-click on the CorelDRAW icon to bring up its main screen.

THE CORELDRAW SCREEN

To access the CorelDRAW's many features, the screen, or desktop, contains many elements. Let's cover all of the elements illustrated in Figure 2.2.

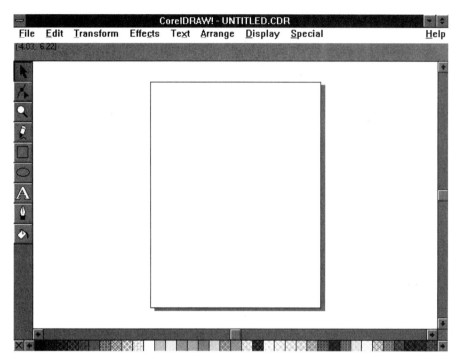

Figure 2.2 *The CorelDRAW screen.*

WINDOWS BORDER AND TITLE BAR

At the very top of the desktop is the Windows border and the title bar.

The Windows border is the same as we saw in Chapter 1, when we reviewed the elements of a window.

At the center of the title bar, you'll see the title of the program, CorelDRAW, and the name of the current file.

Your title bar probably reads *untitled.cdr.* This is because you haven't loaded an existing file or saved the file you are working on. Once you save your drawing as a file and give it a name, the title bar reflects the file name.

THE MENU BAR

The next line contains the menu bar. You will be using these pull-down menus to manage your files, customize and modify your drawings, and tailor your screen display to your individual preferences. In the following chapters, as we proceed through the Toolbox, we'll take a closer look at some of these menu options. Here's a quick overview:

- ▼ **File** controls the files in and out of CorelDRAW and manages printing.
- ▼ **Edit** cuts, copies, and pastes information, and undoes and redoes your previous actions.
- ▼ **Transform** changes the angle, size, rotation, or movement of objects on the screen.
- ▼ **Effects** blends, shapes, envelopes, or adds perspective to objects in your drawing.
- ▼ **Text** aligns or modifies your text, or invokes the spelling-checker or thesaurus.
- ▼ **Arrange** groups images or breaks apart groups of images and changes an object's relative position in a drawing.
- ▼ **Display** provides on-screen aids such as a ruler, a grid, and preview options.
- ▼ **Special** contains miscellaneous options and user preferences.
- ▼ **Help** accesses on-line help for all of the CorelDRAW tools and menu options.

STATUS LINE

The next part of the screen is the status line, which tells you everything you ever wanted to know about the drawing you are currently working on. Let's examine it in detail, as illustrated in Figure 2.3.

Figure 2.3 *The status line.*

The numbers in the upper-left corner of the status line indicate the x and y coordinates of your cursor on the screen. The status line shows the type of selected object, its size, and its location. You may think that this is fairly obvious, but as you go on, you'll see that in a drawing that contains many objects, it is easy to lose track of where you are. The right-hand corner of the status line tells you about the outline and fill of the selected object.

THE TOOLBOX

Along the right-hand side of the screen, you'll see the toolbox, shown in Figure 2.4.

Figure 2.4 *The CorelDRAW toolbox.*

Your toolbox contains icons for drawing tools (lines, rectangles, ellipses, and text), editing tools (select, shape, outline, and fill), and viewing (magnifying) tools.

EDITING WINDOW, PRINTABLE PAGE, AND SCROLL BARS

The large blank portion of the screen is called the *editing window.* You can place objects anywhere within this window, but you can only print objects that are contained on the printable page. CorelDRAW considers anything in the editing window part of the file. If you wish to export the drawing to another format to use it with other software, it exports all of your objects, not just what is on the printable page.

The left and right arrows at the bottom of your screen and the up and down arrows at the right-hand edge of your screen are scroll buttons. They let you view data off the screen when there is more than can fit in the editing window.

Figure 2.5 shows the editing window, the printable page, and the scroll bars.

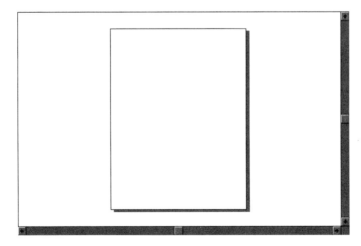

Figure 2.5 *The editing window, printable page, and scroll bars.*

SUMMARY

You're probably anxious to begin creating graphics with CorelDRAW. This chapter has laid the ground work to do just that. You now know how to:

▼ Begin CorelDRAW.

▼ Identify the parts of the CorelDRAW screen.

▼ Recognize the icons in the CorelDRAW toolbox.

▼ Identify the CorelDRAW menu items and know what they are used for.

DRAWING RECTANGLES AND ELLIPSES

This chapter shows you how to use CorelDRAW's tools to create graphics. It also talks about customizing the CorelDRAW desktop to make it easier to create and modify your drawings. Finally, it shows you how to preview your graphics to see how the finished product looks. The topics include:

▼ Customizing your desktop.

▼ Drawing rectangles and squares.

▼ Drawing ellipses and circles.

▼ Full-screen preview.

CUSTOMIZING YOUR DESKTOP

When I first began working with CorelDRAW I couldn't draw a straight line by hand, and I was finding that I couldn't draw it with CorelDRAW either. However, I soon found out that Corel had some helpers for me. When I learned to display rulers and grids, it was easier to align objects on my page and to place my objects correctly. Customize your desktop to make drawing tasks a little easier (and in the process, learn a little about the menus and the dialog boxes).

Click on **Display** on the menu bar. The Display menu in Figure 3.1 appears.

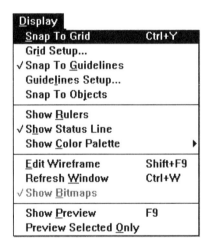

Figure 3.1 *The Display menu.*

This menu customizes your display screen and presents or removes visual aid features. Many of these features are toggles, which means they can only be turned on or off. For these items, simply click on the feature name. If it is on, it clicks off, and if it is off it turns on. An item is turned on when a check mark appears next to it.

SHOW STATUS LINE

Because the status line contains so much helpful information, you'll want to make sure that it is displayed on the screen. If you do not see a check next to this item in the menu, click on **Show Status Line** to turn it on. You'll probably also want to see the color palette at the bottom of your CorelDRAW desktop, so make sure that this item is checked.

SHOW RULERS

Because it is often helpful to be able to see the measurement of the page and the objects on it, you might like to see the rulers on the screen. If Show Rulers (the first menu item in the second grouping) is not checked, click on it. Your CorelDRAW desktop is now displayed with the rulers, color palette, and status line.

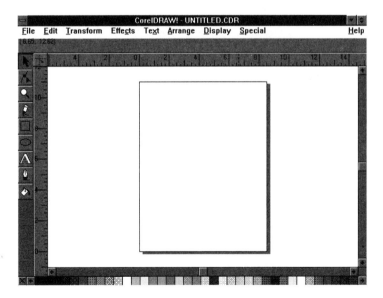

Figure 3.2 *The customized CorelDRAW desktop.*

USING THE GRID

The CorelDRAW grid is another helpful display aid. Along with the rulers, the grid helps you place and space elements of your drawing. However, unlike the rulers, you'll first need to set up your grid and then display it on the screen. Click on **Grid Setup** in the Display menu and a dialog box appears, as shown in Figure 3.3.

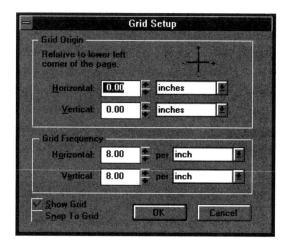

Figure 3.3 *The Grid Setup dialog box.*

The Grid Origin option sets the origin of the grid anywhere in the editing window. The default location is in the lower-left corner of the page. In the measurement units box, you can specify the number of grid points per unit as inches, millimeters, picas, or points. Simply scroll through the measurement types by clicking on the box until the type you want appears in the box.

NOTE The coordinates that you see on the status line reflect the grid origin that you entered.

The Grid Frequency option changes the vertical and horizontal spacing of the grid lines. Again, you can either enter the value or scroll through the numerical values, and also change the measurement types by scrolling through the choices.

The divisions and units on the ruler reflect the selections that you make in the Grid Setup dialog box.

NOTE

Clicking on **Show Grid** shows the unprintable grid marks on the screen. If you click on the **Snap to Grid** checkbox, the objects *snap* to the nearest grid marker whenever you create or move the object. While this feature makes it easier to line up objects, it may also restrict your flexibility. Try it for a while and see if it helps you.

When you're done, click on **OK** to enter your choices and return to the CorelDRAW window.

By now, you're probably anxious to begin drawing, so let's go.

DRAWING RECTANGLES AND SQUARES

To draw rectangles and squares, select the Rectangle tool. There are two methods for doing this:

▼   Click on the Rectangle tool in the Toolbox, or

▼   Press **F6** on your keyboard.

Notice that the Rectangle tool is highlighted, and that your cursor has changed from the outlined arrow to a crosshair.

1. Move the cursor to the printable page and begin drawing your rectangle by holding down the left mouse button and dragging the cursor. An outline shows the position and size of your rectangle as you draw.

2. When the shape is the correct size, release the mouse button.

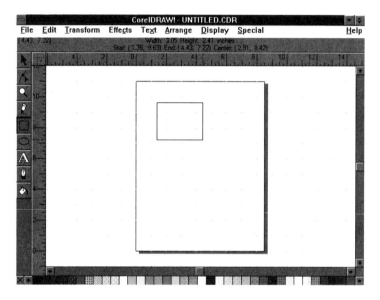

Figure 3.4 *Drawing rectangles.*

 Until you release the mouse button, you can keep changing the size and shape of the rectangle by moving your mouse. You *cannot* change the starting point.

The Rectangle tool also draws squares. This is done much like drawing a rectangle, but by holding down the **Ctrl** key while you drag your mouse. Your shape is constrained to a square.

 Do not release the **Ctrl** key before you release the mouse button. If you do, your shape will be a rectangle, not a square.

When you drew the rectangle and square, you began at one of the outside corners and dragged the mouse to the opposite corner. You can also draw a rectangle from the inside out.

1. Move your cursor to the point on the screen where you want the center of the shape.
2. While pressing the **Shift** key, click and drag in either direction. The rectangle forms from the center point that you designated.

You can also draw a square from the center point out by pressing both the **Ctrl** and **Shift** keys while clicking and dragging the mouse.

If you don't like the way your rectangle or square looks, select it and press the **Del** key to erase it .

NOTE

DRAWING ELLIPSES AND CIRCLES

Use the same technique to draw ellipses and circles as you did to draw rectangles and squares. Select the Ellipse tool by using one of these two methods:

▼ Click on the Ellipse tool in the Toolbox, or
▼ Press **F7** on your keyboard.

The Ellipse tool is highlighted, and the cursor changes from the arrow to a crosshair.

1. Move the cursor to the printable page where you want to begin drawing your ellipse.
2. Click and drag the cursor in the direction in which you want to draw the ellipse.
3. When the shape is the correct size, release the mouse button.

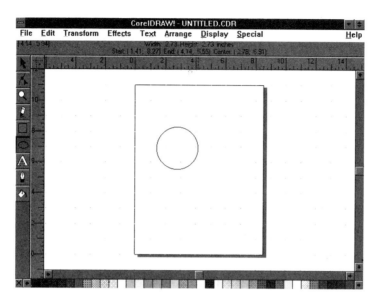

Figure 3.5 *Drawing an ellipse.*

N O T E   Until you release the mouse button, you can keep changing the size and shape of the ellipse by moving your mouse. You *cannot* change the starting point.

To draw a perfect circle, press the **Ctrl** key while you are dragging the mouse. Do not release the **Ctrl** key before you release the mouse button or your shape will be a ellipse, not a circle.

When you drew the ellipse and the circle, you began at one of the outside corners and dragged the mouse to the opposite corner. You can also draw an ellipse from the inside out.

1. Move your cursor to the point on the screen where you want to center the shape.

2. Press the **Shift** key, hold down the mouse button and drag the cursor. The ellipse forms on both sides of the center point you designated.

To draw a perfect circle from the inside out, simultaneously press the **Ctrl** and **Shift** keys while clicking and dragging your mouse. You'll see a circle "growing" from your center point outward.

You can erase an ellipse or circle by simply selecting it and pressing the **Del** key.

Before moving on, draw a few rectangles, squares, ellipses, and circles. This gives you some good practice working with the mouse, as well as with your keyboard. While working with these shapes, observe a few things.

1. The status line reflects your current cursor location, as well as the size, shape, and center of your object.

2. The currently selected object has tiny squares at the corner points (if it is a rectangle or square), or one somewhere on the curve (if it is a circle or ellipse). These are *nodes*, which you will use later while you're modifying, shaping, and editing your drawings. They don't appear in your final (or printed) copy.

FULL-SCREEN PREVIEW

Use a full-screen preview to see what this practice page looks like. Select **Display** from the Main menu bar, and select **Show Full Screen Preview**. Pressing **F9** also gives you a full-screen preview, as shown in Figure 3.6. Pressing **F9** again returns your screen to its normal CorelDRAW format, also known as the *wire screen*.

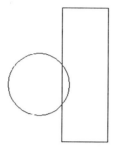

Figure 3.6 Full-screen preview.

SUMMARY

You now know how to:

- ▼ Customize your desktop.
- ▼ Draw circles, ellipses, rectangle, and squares.
- ▼ Preview your graphics.

The shortcuts explained in this chapter are:

- ▼ **F6** Rectangle.
- ▼ **F7** Ellipse.
- ▼ **F9** Full-screen preview.

DRAWING LINES AND CURVES

You would quickly find yourself limited if rectangles and ellipses were the only drawing tools available to you. Fortunately, CorelDRAW provides a Pencil tool for drawing lines and curves. This chapter cover:

▼ Drawing straight lines.

▼ Drawing curves.

▼ Moving and Modifying objects.

▼ Undo, Redo, Delete, and Duplicate.

▼ Creating a drawing.

DRAWING STRAIGHT LINES

Don't worry if you've never been able to draw straight lines by hand. With CorelDRAW, anyone can. Click on the Pencil icon in the toolbox. The cursor changes from an arrow and the Pencil icon becomes highlighted. Check the status line—you'll see that you're drawing in freehand mode. The Pencil tool also draws in Bezier mode. These two methods work in very much the same way when drawing straight lines, but as you'll soon see, they operate very differently when creating curves.

SHORT CUT

Press **F5** to activate the Pencil tool.

FREEHAND LINES

To draw a straight line in freehand mode:

1. Position the cursor wherever you want your line to begin, then click and release the mouse button. (Be sure to release the mouse button before moving the cursor or you will draw a curve instead of a straight line.).

2. Move your cursor until the line is at the angle and length that you want, and click the mouse button again. Before you click the button, however, play with your cursor a bit. Watch how easy it is to swing your line upwards, downwards, or even backwards to shorten the line again.

3. When the line is exactly as you want it, click the mouse, and a straight line appears. The two small squares at each end of the line designate the node point.

Figure 4.1 *Drawing in freehand mode.*

You can also restrict (constrain) the angle of your line as you draw. Try doing another line, but this time, constrain the angle of the line to 15 degrees.

1. With the pencil tool still selected, press the **Ctrl** key before you click the mouse.

2. Hold the **Ctrl** key while you extend the line upward and outward from the starting point.

3. As you move your cursor, you'll notice that the line does not swing freely, but instead, jumps in even increments. These are 15-degree angles.

4. When the line is where you want it, click the mouse button and only then release the **Ctrl** key.

If you release the **Ctrl** key before you click the mouse, the line does not remain constrained to the 15-degree angle.

To practice what you've just learned, keep drawing lines (with the **Ctrl** key depressed) in 15-degree angles around a center point, until you've drawn a starburst of lines.

JOINING FREEHAND LINES

You can also use the Pencil tool to create a series of joined lines, with each one beginning where the previous one left off. To practice, draw a row of zig-zag lines across the page.

1. Choose a blank spot anywhere on the left side of your page and click the mouse.

2. Move to an ending point up and to the right and double-click. This location becomes the end point of the first line, and the beginning point of the second line.

3. Move the cursor down and to the right, and double-click. You've ended the second line, and begun the third.

4. Continue drawing lines in this manner, until you have a zig-zag pattern across the page.

Figure 4.2 *Several joined freehand lines.*

CLEARING THE SCREEN

Let's get a little more practice with drawing freehand lines before we move on to the next method. Clear the page so it will be easier to see what you're doing.

1. Open the File menu and click on **New**.

2. Before clearing the screen, CorelDRAW checks to see if you really want to save the current drawing. Click on **NO**, and your editable and printable page is be cleared.

Now, draw a five-pointed star made of five lines.

1. Choose a blank spot on your screen and click your mouse to begin.

2. Choose the second point and double-click.

3. Bring the cursor back down and double-click again. The first "point" of the star is complete.

4. Proceed until you've drawn all five points as shown in Figure 4.3. You may also want to try this with the **Ctrl** key pressed to constrain the angles.

If you don't like your star, press **Del** to erase it. If you only want to delete a part of it, press **Alt-Backspace** (a keyboard shortcut for Undo) to wipe out only the last segment that you drew.

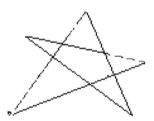

Figure 4.3 *Drawing a star.*

BEZIER LINES

To see how drawing lines works in Bezier mode, hold down the mouse button while you click on the Pencil tool, and you'll see a pop-up menu displaying the freehand and Bezier icons.

Figure 4.4 *The freehand and Bezier drawing mode icons.*

The icon that looks like the Pencil tool indicates freehand mode. The icon that looks like a Pencil with a dashed line underneath represents Bezier mode.

When you select Bezier mode, your toolbox reflects your choice by displaying the Bezier pencil.

NOTE

To draw a line in Bezier mode, do it exactly as you did before:

1. Click on a starting point.
2. Move your cursor to the line's ending point.

3. Click the mouse again to complete the line. The status line reminds you that you are in Bezier mode. Another item to note on the status line is that, although you drew a line, the status line indicates that you drew a curve.

JOINED BEZIER LINES

You'll find that there's a difference when drawing multisegment lines in Bezier mode. To try it, clear your screen.

1. Draw a single line anywhere on the page, but only single click at the end of the line.

2. Move your cursor anywhere else on the editable page and click once. A second line is drawn from the end of the first line to the point that you just clicked on.

3. For practice, try redrawing the five-pointed star in Bezier mode.

As you can see, there's very little difference between these two methods when drawing straight lines.

DRAWING CURVES

Drawing curves is very different in Freehand and Bezier modes, so now is a good time to examine the differences between these two modes of drawing.

▼ **Freehand curves** are drawn along the path defined with your mouse, somewhat like the way you would draw curves by hand.

▼ **Bezier curves** are placed precisely between two defined points (nodes), resulting in a smoother curve.

FREEHAND CURVES

Make sure that your screen is cleared and check your status line to see that you are in Freehand mode.

1. Move the cursor to a beginning point for your curve and press and hold the mouse button.

2. While holding the mouse button, move the cursor, tracing the path the curve will follow.

Figure 4.5 *Drawing a freehand curve.*

Check the status line. You'll notice that the curve is identified, with the number of nodes in the curve. At the right side of the screen, you'll also see that the curve is identified as an open path (as opposed to a closed figure, like a rectangle or an ellipse).

To create a closed curve, simply make sure that the beginning and end points meet. The status line will no longer show the figure as an open path.

To erase the entire curve, either press the **Del** key or **Alt-Backspace**. To erase only a portion of the curve while you're drawing it, hold down the **Shift** key while backtracking over the portion of the curve you want to erase.

Just as you drew multi-segment lines, you can draw multisegment curves with the Pencil tool. To begin a multisegment curve:

1. Draw a curve on the screen.

2. Without moving the cursor from the point where you end the first curve, click to begin the second curve and then sketch it out.

3. When you complete the second curve, it snaps to the first, closing any gap between the two.

Figure 4.6 *Drawing mulitsegment freehand curves.*

BEZIER CURVES

Unless you're extremely coordinated (or have done this before) you may be feeling somewhat frustrated by now, because your curves have a nursery school quality to them. Curves in Bezier mode draw more smoothly and precisely, but it may take a little practice.

In Bezier mode, you place a node, specify control points that designate the height and depth of the curve, then place the next node. Between the two nodes, CorelDRAW places a curve reflecting the control points you specified.

Let's try drawing some curves. First, check your status line to make sure you're in Bezier mode.

1. Select a point somewhere at the middle of your page, and press the mouse button. A node (a small filled box) is displayed

2. Move your mouse until the control points (two small boxes connected to the node by a dashed line) are displayed.

3. Drag a control point in the direction that you want the curve to take. Dragging away from the node increases the height and depth. Dragging towards the node decreases the height and depth.

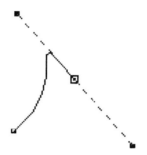

Figure 4.7 *Dragging the control points of a Bezier curve.*

To change the slope of the curve, rotate the control points around the node.

Keep dragging your node until you have drawn a rough circle.

While you are working on this page, practice drawing other curves. You can make open curves, curves with loops in them, or closed curves. The more you work with drawing different types of curves in Bezier mode, the more skillful you'll become at controlling the curves. As you make your curves, watch the grid and rulers. These tools make it easier to place your nodes and fix the height and slope of your curves.

AUTOJOIN

If it's important to join lines and curves together, you may want to adjust the AutoJoin parameter. Click on the Special menu and select **Preferences**.

From the dialog box shown, select **Curves**, click on **AutoJoin** and set the number to 10.

This forces two separated end nodes of one object to join when they are 10 pixels apart or less. The default setting is, 5. A lower AutoJoin number prevents nodes from automatically joining unless you draw them very precisely—a larger number is more forgiving.

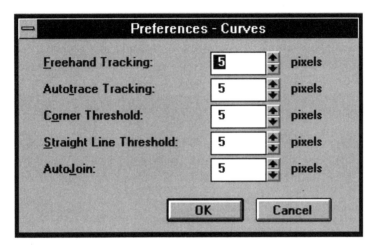

Figure 4.8 *Setting the AutoJoin parameters in the Preferences-Curves dialog box.*

MOVING AND MODIFYING OBJECTS

The Pick tool, the arrow icon at the top of the toolbox, is very powerful. When selected, this tool lets you move, size, scale, and rotate any object on your screen.

Before using this tool, let's create a page that we can work with. Clear the current screen and draw a few objects, perhaps a rectangle, a circle, a line, and a curve.

MOVING OBJECTS

Follow these steps to move objects:

1. Click on the Pick tool.

Press the **Spacebar** to select the Pick tool after creating any object (except text).

2. Move your cursor to the rectangle that you have drawn on your page and press the mouse button. A dotted rectangle is displayed, representing the object that you're about to move.

3. Drag the dotted rectangle anywhere on the page.

4. When you are satisfied with the new location, release the mouse button, and the line is displayed in its new location.

Practice moving the different objects around the page until you're confident that you can place them exactly in their new locations.

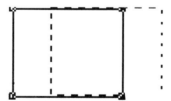

Figure 4.9 *Moving objects.*

You can also select **Move** from the Transform menu to move your objects. You may want to move an object this way if you know exactly where you want it to go, or you want to move it a given distance from its present location.

1. Select the object that you want to move, and click on **Move** in the Transform menu.

2 In the dialog box, enter the distance that you want to move the object in the Horizontal and Vertical fields. You can also change the units by clicking in the scroll box to view and change your selection.

3. To leave a copy of the original (in other words, create a duplicate), click on the **Leave Original** checkbox.

You can also enter an exact coordinate location in the Horizontal or Vertical field. You'll need to determine the coordinates of the new location before you select the object and enter the Move dialog box. Use the grid and rulers to help you.

RESHAPING OBJECTS

The Pick tool also reshapes objects. With Pick selected, click on any outer edge of an object. You'll see eight small black boxes, called *handles*, displayed around the object. Use these handles to stretch, shrink, or scale an object.

Select the rectangle on your page.

STRETCHING OBJECTS

Stretch the rectangle horizontally.

1. Move your cursor over one of the handles on the vertical edge of the rectangle until the cursor becomes a crosshair.

2. Click and hold the mouse button. When the dotted rectangle appears, drag outward with your mouse. Watch the side of the rectangle that you selected stretch outward.

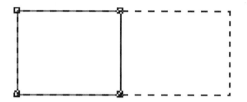

Figure 4.10 *Stretching an object.*

You can also stretch an object by using the Transform menu. Click on **Stretch & Mirror**.

Enter the percentage that you want to stretch the object, vertically and or horizontally. For example, if you enter 50 percent in the horizontal box and 0 percent in the vertical box, the image will be half as wide, but the same height. You can choose to mirror the object either horizontally or vertically. You can also leave a copy of the original by clicking on the **Leave Original** checkbox.

SHRINKING OBJECTS

You can also shrink an object in much the same way.

1. With the rectangle still selected, move the cursor over one of the handles on the horizontal edge of the rectangle until it becomes a crosshair.
2. Click the mouse button.
3. When the dotted rectangle appears, drag inward. The side of the rectangle that you selected shrinks inward.

SCALING OBJECTS

So far you've used the Pick tool to resize the object, but it was not resized proportionally—the rectangle no longer has the same proportions as it did when you first drew it.

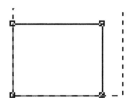

Figure 4.11 *Shrinking an object.*

1. Click on the circle.

2. When the handles appear, move your cursor to one of the corner handles until it becomes a crosshair.

3. Press the mouse button and the dotted rectangle is displayed.

4. As you drag outward, the circle stretches slowly in the direction that you move the mouse. The circle is being stretched in increments that maintain its proportions, the ratio of width to height..

While you are stretching, shrinking, or scaling an object, you can create a copy of the original object.

1. Select the curve that you drew, and put your cursor on one of the handles.

2. Stretch the object while simultaneously pressing the + key on the numeric keyboard.

3. When you're done, release both the mouse button and the + key. You'll see your stretched object as well as a copy of the original object.

ROTATING, SKEWING, AND MIRRORING OBJECTS

You can also use the Pick tool to rotate or skew an object.

ROTATING OBJECTS

Follow these steps to rotate an object:

1. Move your cursor to the rectangle on your page and double-click on any edge of the object. You'll see a series of double-headed arrows appear around the rectangle.

2. Move the cursor to one of the curved double arrows at a *corner* until the cursor becomes a crosshair.

3. Press the mouse button and the dotted rectangle is displayed.

4. Drag it in the direction you want to rotate the rectangle. You'll notice a small horseshoe shape with an arrow on each end just below the rectangle.

5. When you've rotated the blue rectangle to the location and direction that you want, release the mouse button.

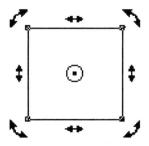

Figure 4.12 Rotating an object.

While you are rotating an object, you can control, or constrain, the angle of rotation. Hold the **Ctrl** key while dragging the object and the object rotates in increments of 15 degrees.

If you press the **+** key on the numeric keypad while rotating the object, a copy of the original remains on the screen.

SKEWING OBJECTS

When the double-headed arrows are around your object, you can also skew it. Unlike rotating, which maintains the same shape but simply turns it around, skewing pulls the object in a direction, slanting it either horizontally or vertically.

To skew an object:

1. Move the cursor over one of the top, bottom, or side handles until it changes to a crosshair.
2. Drag the object in the direction you wish to skew it. The dotted highlighting box skews as you drag the cursor.
3. When the dotted outline is the shape you want, release the mouse button.

While rotating or skewing an object, use the **Ctrl** key to constrain the amount of rotation. Don't forget using the **+** key leaves the original behind as before.

MIRRORING OBJECTS

You can also flip an object to create a mirror image of an object.

1. Select one of the objects that you just rotated.
2. Drag one of the side handles back across the object while holding the **Ctrl** key, and a mirror image of the object is displayed.

The **Ctrl** key, constrains the image to increments of 100 percent of its original size while mirroring. Without the **Ctrl** key, your image will not be truly mirrored, since it will be a different size than the original. You can mirror an object while leaving the original by also pressing the **+** key on the numeric keyboard while dragging back across the object.

To mirror vertically, select the top or bottom middle handle and drag the handle through the object.

You can also rotate and skew any object on your screen using the Transform menu.

1. Select the object you wish to rotate or skew, and click on **Rotate & Skew** in the Transform menu.
2. To rotate the object, enter a value in the Rotation Angle box.
3. To skew an object, enter a value in the Skew Horizontally and/or Skew Vertically box.
4. Create a duplicate by clicking on the **Leave Original** checkbox.

UNDO, REDO, DELETE, AND DUPLICATE

There are several handy options on the Edit menu that can help you manage the objects on your screen.

If you select **Undo** from the Edit menu, CorelDRAW undoes the last command or action that you performed. In other words, if you moved, stretched, scaled, or rotated an object, and you don't like the results of the last action, select **Undo**.

Press **Alt-Backspace** to perform an Undo.

If you change your mind again, select **Redo** from the Edit menu, and CorelDRAW undoes the undo.

Select the Delete option from the Edit menu to erase an object from the screen as an alternative to pressing the **Del** key.

Use the Edit menu to create a duplicate of an object on the screen. With an object selected, select **Duplicate** from the Edit menu, and a duplicate copy of the object is displayed. The duplicate is placed in a position from the original as defined in the Preferences menu.

Press **Ctrl-D** to create a duplicate of the object.

SHORT CUT

CREATING A DRAWING

You've learned enough of the basics of CorelDRAW to create a simple drawing. Before you do so, clear your page.

This drawing is the beginning of a simple beach poster. First, draw a beach chair on the left side of the page.

1. Select the Rectangle tool, and halfway down the left side of the page, draw a horizontal rectangle. This forms the back of your director's chair.

2. About 1.5 inches down, draw a narrow horizontal rectangle, of the same width, then connect the two rectangles with a line on either side.

3. Put some legs on the chair. Select the Ellipse tool. Starting at the bottom of the lower rectangle, draw a narrow, ellipse.

4. Press the **Spacebar** to select the Pick tool. (The ellipse will still be selected.) Double-click on one of the boxes until the rotate arrows appear, then rotate the ellipse until it is in a diagonal position.

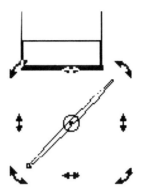

Figure 4.14 *The beach chair takes shape.*

5. Create a duplicate mirror image of the narrow ellipse. While holding the **+** key on the numeric keypad, drag one of the side handles around the ellipse back over the ellipse. You'll see a mirrored duplicate of the ellipse. Move the two ellipses until they form the crossed legs of the director's chair, and you've created your first graphic.

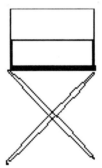

Figure 4.15 *Your first graphic—a beach chair.*

6. Before we continue our beach poster, save what you've done so far. From the File menu, select **Save**. The Save Drawing dialog box is displayed.

7. Be sure you are pointing to the directory where you want to save your drawing. In the box provided, key in the file name you want. Let's call this drawing BEACH.

All CorelDRAW files will automatically have the standard *.CDR file extension attached.

N O T E

8. Click on **OK**. CorelDRAW returns to the drawing page. Note that an hourglass appears while the file is being written to disk.

9. To continue drawing the poster, add a beach ball in the extreme lower-left corner of the page. Select the Ellipse tool, and while you drag with your mouse, hold the **Ctrl** key to form a circle. Add another small circle at approximately the center of the larger one, and you have the outlines of your beach ball.

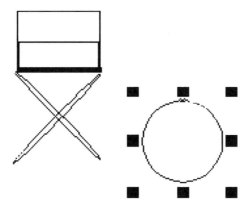

Figure 4.16 *The outline of a beach ball.*

10. Finish the beach ball by selecting the Pencil tool and adding some curves. You can do these in either freehand or Bezier mode, but you'll have more control over your lines if you use Bezier mode.

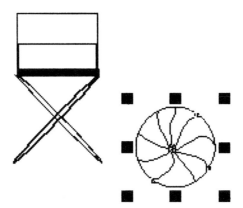

Figure 4.17 *The completed beach ball.*

11. To complete our poster (at least for the time being), let's tie a kite to the chair. Select the Rectangle tool, and in the upper-left corner, draw a rectangle. Rotate it, skew it, then stretch it, until it forms a diamond shape.

12. With the Pencil tool selected, add horizontal and diagonal lines across the body of the kite. Then create a curve to "tie" the kite to the arm of the director's chair.

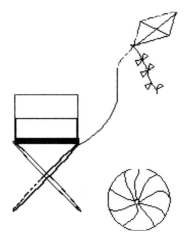

Figure 4.18 *The beach poster with a kite.*

In the next chapter, we'll work with the Outline and Fill tools to spruce up our poster. In the meantime, though, let's save our file. From the File menu, select **Save** and the file is automatically saved on disk, with the name that you assigned before.

SUMMARY

In this chapter, you've learned about lines and curves, some of the basic building blocks in CorelDRAW. You've also seen how to use the Pick tool (as well as the Transform menu) to modify, move, and manipulate objects. You have accomplished the following:

▼ Drawing freehand lines and curves.

▼ Drawing Bezier lines and curves.

▼ Using the Pick tool and the Transform menu to:

♦ Move objects.

♦ Stretch, shrink, and scale objects.

♦ Rotate, skew, and mirror objects.

▼ Using the Edit menu to:

♦ Undo or Redo previous actions.

♦ Delete or Duplicate objects on your screen.

▼ Using the File menu to:

♦ Clear the screen.

♦ Save drawings.

▼ Creating a drawing.

FILLING AND OUTLINING OBJECTS

Art and graphics would be pretty boring if they were simple line drawings, so this chapter covers:

▼ The Fill tool.

▼ The Outline tool.

THE FILL TOOL

The Fill tool is displayed on your tool bar as a bucket of paint. To fill an object, select the object, then click on the Fill tool. A fly-out menu showing the various fill options is displayed.

SHORT CUT

Press **F11** to select the Fill tool.

Let's define the items on the fly-out menu (from left to right, top to bottom).

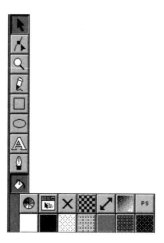

Figure 5.1 The Fill tool fly-out menu.

▼ **Uniform Color Fill**, represented by a color wheel, selects a uniform color to fill your object.

▼ **Roll-Up Fill**, represented by a small menu, activates the Fill roll-up menu, which contains many of the options from the fill fly-out menu.

A roll-up menu is a dialog box that remains on the screen all of the time, but can be rolled up to keep your screen uncluttered. There's an up arrow in the upper-right corner of the menu, and a minus sign in the upper-left corner. Once you've accessed and used a roll-up, simply click on the up arrow to roll it up and out of the way, much the same way as you'd roll up a window shade. The title bar remains visible. When you need the dialog box again, click on the minus sign and the roll-up is restored.

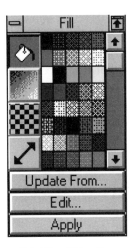

Figure 5.2 *The Fill roll-up menu.*

- ▼ **No Fill**, represented by an X, creates an object with no fill. If there are other objects under one that is unfilled, they show through.

- ▼ **Two-Color Pattern**, represented by a checkerboard square, to fill your object with a two-color pattern.

- ▼ **Color Pattern**, represented by a diagonal, double-headed arrow, allows you to access full-color patterns and select one to fill your object.

- ▼ **Fountain Fill,** a shaded color blend from one color to another, is available by selecting the shaded box.

▼ **Post Script Texture** selects PostScript effects, if you are using a PostScript printer.

▼ **Shades of Gray** (white, black, and 5 shades of gray) are available from the bottom row of the fill fly-out menu.

You can only fill closed objects. An open path must be closed before you can fill it.

N O T E

COLOR FILL

Let's start by choosing some uniform color fill for our beach ball. Make sure that the object is selected, then click on the color wheel. If there are no objects selected, the Uniform Fill for New Object dialog box is displayed. This dialog box sets the defaults for objects being created.

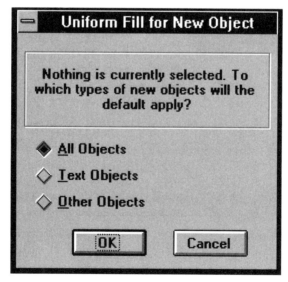

Figure 5.3 *The Uniform Fill for New Object dialog box.*

You can click on any of the three options shown then click on **OK** to confirm or click on **Cancel**, which allows you to return to the page and click the correct object.

Choose a bright red from the palette. (Click on the Palette button if the palette is not displayed.) Click on the color and the beach ball will be filled in. Choose another color and fill the kite.

You can create your own colors by "mixing" the process inks—cyan, magenta, yellow, and black. There are many guide wheels and books available to help you determine what percentages of these inks create the colors you want.

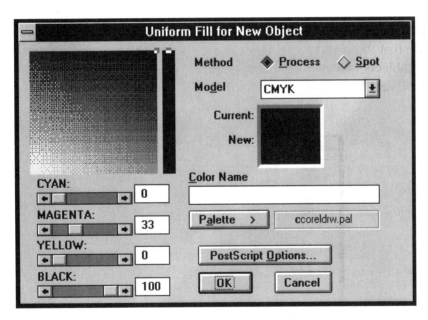

Figure 5.4 Creating process colors.

You can also fill an object using the Fill roll-up. Click on the roll-up menu (or restore it, if it's already on your screen). Click on the paint bucket, and a color palette is displayed. Click on the color you want to apply color to the object.

PATTERNS

TWO-COLOR PATTERNS

To fill your object with a two-color pattern, select the checkerboard square icon. A Two-Color Pattern dialog box is displayed.

To view all of the patterns, click on the small gray arrow on the bottom-right corner of the pattern display box of the roll-up menu. Use the scroll arrow to see all the patterns. Click on the one that you want to use and it is displayed in the preview box.

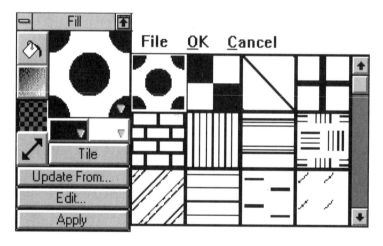

Figure 5.5 *Choosing a two-color pattern.*

You can choose small, medium, and large versions of your pattern. Change the size of the small, medium, and large tiles using the height and width boxes.

The Back and Front options change the background and foreground colors. As you change the selections, you'll see the preview box change.

Patterns are made up of tiles, and you can stagger them in the same way that you arrange tiles on a floor or a wall. CorelDRAW lets you change the way the individual tiles in your pattern repeat. Click on **Tiling** in the roll-up menu and you'll see a detailed dialog box. Select **Create** to make your own patterns.

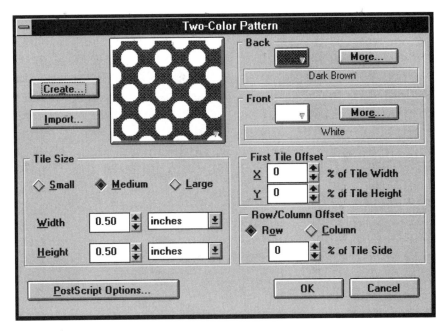

Figure 5.6 *The Tiling dialog box.*

Changing the first tile offset shifts the entire pattern either horizontally or vertically. The Row/Column offset changes the offset within an individual repetition.

Let's go back to our beach drawing, and choose a tiled two-color pattern for the back of our director's chair.

FULL-COLOR PATTERNS

The Full-Color Pattern option, accessible from the fly-out or the roll-up menus, works in a similar way as the two-color pattern. Full-color patterns are vector graphics.

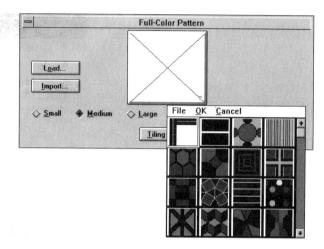

Figure 5.7 *Full-color pattern choices.*

FOUNTAIN FILL

A fountain fill is a blend or tint from one color to another that gives a shaded effect. Select a fountain fill from the fly-out menu or the roll-up window.

The fountain fill shown in the preview box has a *linear fill,* which means that the fill occurs in a particular direction, determined by the angle that you specify.

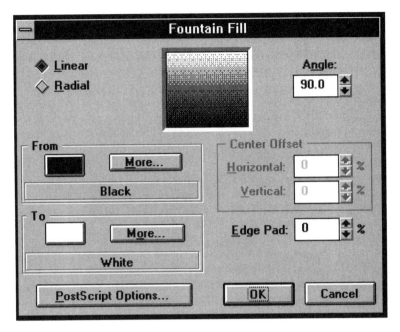

Figure 5.8 *The Fountain Fill dialog box.*

A *radial fill* radiates from the center outward . The center point may be moved to create a point of light by specifying a Center Offset.

You can change the colors of the fountain fill by clicking on the **More** box in the From or To portion of the dialog box.

Let's change the beach ball to a radial fountain fill to give it a feeling of depth. If you have a PostScript printer, you can use the PS option, and choose from a variety of available halftone screens.

POSTSCRIPT TEXTURES

PostScript printer owners may also choose from a list of PostScript textures (an earlier version of patterns). These patterns appear in printed pieces, but not on screen. On screen, objects fill with the letters *PS*. Samples of these textures are available in your CorelDRAW documentation.

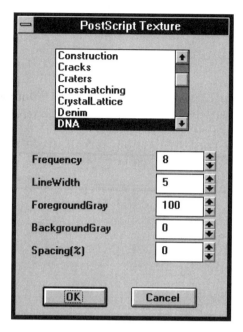

Figure 5.9 The PostScript textures dialog box.

BLACK-AND-WHITE FILL

If you are drawing or printing in simple black and white, use the bottom
row of fill patterns, which allows you to choose from black, white, and
five shades of gray for your graphics.

Let's choose a medium-gray fill for the legs of the director's chair.

Save your drawing by selecting **Save** from the File menu.

THE OUTLINE TOOL

The Outline tool is displayed on your tool bar as a pen nib. To change an outline, select the object, then click on the Outline tool. A fly-out menu showing the various outline options is displayed.

Press **F12** to select the Outline tool.

SHORT CUT

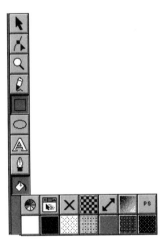

Figure 5.10 The Outline tool fly-out menu.

Select the Penpoint from this menu to choose the default outline style for your objects. If no object is currently selected, you can make a selection from the dialog box shown to set new defaults.

The next item selects the Outline roll-up menu.

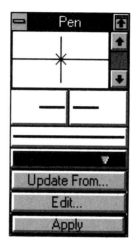

Figure 5.11 *The Outline roll-up menu.*

As with the Fill roll-up menu, you can make many of your outline selections from this window.

OUTLINE WIDTH

The remainder of the selections on the top row of the fly-out menu allow you to choose the outline thickness (including X for no outline). You may want to experiment with these to find out which outline size will best enhance your object. Choose a wide outline for the two supports of the director's chair (connecting the back to the seat), and let's take a look at how the beach poster is shaping up.

OUTLINE COLOR

Using the options on the bottom row of the outline flyout menu, you can also choose a shade of gray or a color for your outline.

For now, however, select an object and return to the pen nib option and examine the Outline pen options.

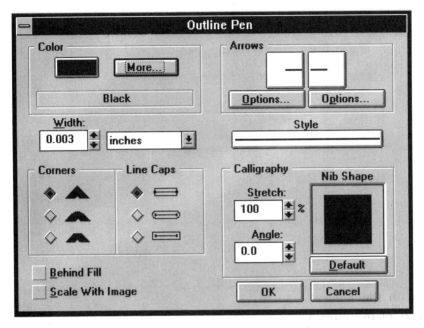

Figure 5.12 *The Outline Pen dialog box.*

You can make several selections from this dialog box to show how your outlines will look.

The upper-left corner of the dialog box selects an outline's color. To see what is available, click on **More** and make your selection. You can also alter the size (and the units) of the outline with the Width Numeric Entry and Variable Units boxes.

Below these are two groups of radio buttons that select the corner and line cap styles for your outlines. Beside each checkbox, the option is visually shown.

You can also place your outlines *behind* the fill of an object, using the checkbox at the bottom of the screen. Placing the outline behind the fill makes the outline appear thinner.

Another checkbox at the bottom of the screen scales the outline with an object, changing the outline's thickness. For example, if you enlarge an object, the outline also becomes thicker.

One of the more powerful outline tools is the ability to choose a type of line ending by selecting the corner style and line caps. In the top right side of the dialog box (or the top half of the roll-up) are two arrow preview boxes. Click on the line end you wish to select (beginning or end) and a selection of arrowheads is displayed.

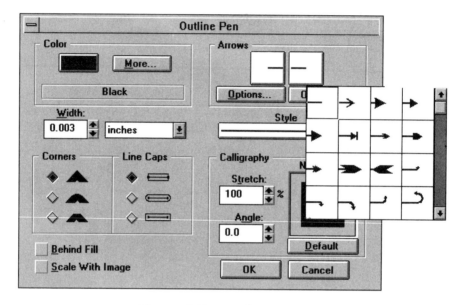

Figure 5.13 *Arrowhead selection.*

Make a selection, and the preview box reflects your choice.

If you do not see the arrowhead you want, tailor an existing one to your needs. Select **Options**, then select **Edit**. Using the Arrowhead Editor, you can perform some basic editing on an arrowhead.

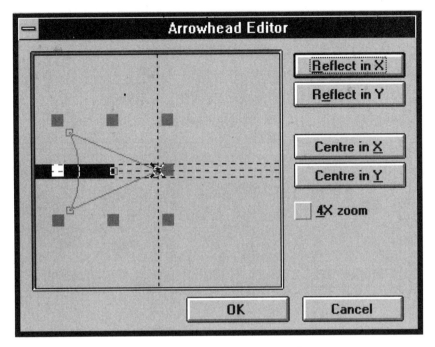

Figure 5.14 *The Arrowhead Editor.*

LINE STYLES

Another selection you can make from the Outline Pen dialog box is the line style. Click on the line preview box under style, and a variety of choices, including dotted and dashed lines, is displayed.

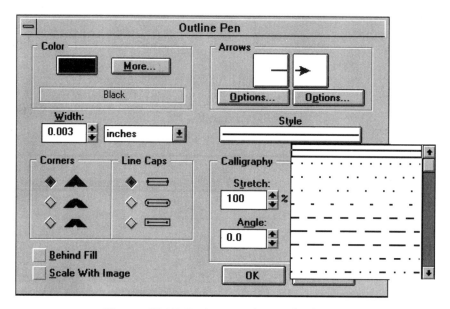

Figure 15.15 *Outline pen line style choices.*

You can create a calligraphic outline by changing the stretch, angle and rotation of the nib.

SUMMARY

In this chapter, you have seen how easy it is to outline and fill any CorelDRAW object. You've learned how to:

▼ Use a CorelDRAW roll-up menu.

▼ Fill any closed object with color.

▼ Use a two-color or full-color pattern fill.

▼ Fill with black, white, or shades of gray.

▼ Choose a fountain fill.

▼ Select line thickness for outlines.

▼ Choose and edit ends, such as arrowheads, for lines and outlines.

▼ Change your line style to dotted or dashed.

Now that you've learned how to add some exciting special effects to graphics with fills and outlines, you're ready to refine drawings by shaping lines and curves.

SHAPING OBJECTS

CorelDRAW places nodes on objects, as we saw when we drew lines and curves. These nodes are used to change the shape of objects.

This chapter covers:

▼ Shaping rectangles and ellipses.
▼ The Zoom tool.
▼ Shaping lines and curves.

SHAPING RECTANGLES AND ELLIPSES

The easiest shaping tasks that you can perform in CorelDRAW are shaping rectangles and ellipses. So, before we begin learning about the Shape tool, put a few rectangles and ellipses on the screen.

SHAPING RECTANGLES

Click on the Shape tool. You'll notice that the cursor changes from a crosshair to a filled arrowhead. Use this cursor to select a rectangle on your page.

A rectangle (or a square) has a node in each corner. Select any of these nodes and drag it around the corner.

When you click on a node, it changes from hollow to filled. When you drag the node the corners become rounded. The corners of the rectangle have now been changed to curves.

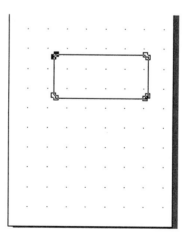

Figure 6.1 *Dragging a node of a rectangle with the Shape tool.*

If, later on, you choose the Pick tool to stretch, shrink, or skew a rectangle you've already shaped, the curved corners or the rectangle stretch, shrink, or skew along with the rest of the rectangle.

SHAPING ELLIPSES

The Shape tool can create arcs or pie wedges from ellipses and circles. Select the **Shape** tool and use the shape cursor (the black arrowhead) to select an ellipse. Place the arrowhead on the ellipse's single node.

To create an *arc* from the ellipse, click and drag the mouse in a circle with the cursor outside the ellipse. As you drag the mouse, you'll see the node split in two.

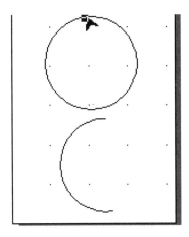

Figure 6.2 Dragging the node of an ellipse with the Shape tool.

When the arc is the length that you want, release the mouse button.

The status line shows the location of the two new nodes, as well as the angle created between them.

N O T E

To create a *wedge* from the ellipse, select the **Shape** tool, then select another ellipse or circle to shape. Again, click on the single node, and click and drag the mouse. However, instead of dragging along the outside of the outline, drag the node with the cursor *inside* the ellipse or circle, as in figure 6.3.

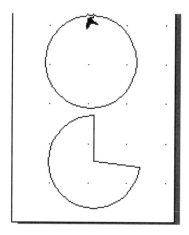

Figure 6.3 *Using the Shape tool to make a wedge.*

Again, the status line shows the location of the two new nodes, as well as the angle between the nodes.

THE ZOOM TOOL

Sometimes when you are working on an object, you might find it difficult to see clearly the section you want to change. Particularly when you're using the Shape tool to work with curves with multiple nodes, you may need a close-up view of one or two of the nodes. To help you focus on what you need to see (or to expand it to get the big picture), CorelDRAW has a Zoom tool, the third item on the tool bar.

When you click on the Zoom tool, a fly-out menu offers five options, as in figure 6.4.

Figure 6.4 The Zoom tool fly-out menu.

ZOOM IN

The first option, Zoom In, displays a magnifying glass with the plus sign. When you select Zoom In, the cursor becomes a magnifying glass. Click and drag the mouse over the portion of the page you want to magnify.

SHORT CUT

Press **F2** to select the Zoom In tool.

If you think that you'll frequently need the zoom-in feature, you can program your right mouse button to zoom in. From the Special menu, choose **Preferences**. From the Preferences dialog box, shown in Figure 6.5, select **Mouse**, and the mouse dialog box is displayed.

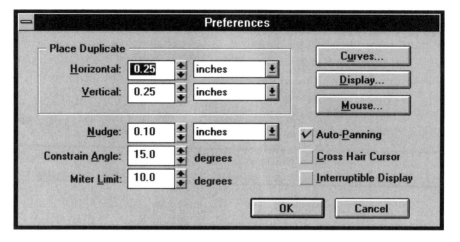

Figure 6.5 *The Preferences dialog box.*

There are several options for programming the right mouse button. Select the feature that you think you'll use most often, click on its check box, and click on **OK**.

ZOOM OUT

Zoom Out, shown as a magnifying glass with a minus sign, reduces magnification back to the previous zoom level.

Press **F3** to zoom out one magnification level. Remember, however, that you can keep zooming out until your page is smaller than the original.

ACTUAL SIZE

The third option, 1:1, displays the objects on your screen as close as possible to the size they will appear on the printed page.

FIT IN WINDOW

Fit in Window changes the magnification so that everything you've drawn, whether or not it fits on the printable page, is displayed.

This is useful if you import into CorelDRAW an object that is larger than the CorelDRAW window and you need to select it to resize it.

NOTE

SHOW PAGE

Show Page changes the magnification so that the entire printable page is displayed.

Press **F4** to execute Show Page.

SHORT CUT

Remember that while you're zoomed in, you still have access to your entire graphic. Use the scroll bars at the top and sides of your screen to move the drawing in the window.

SHAPING LINES AND CURVES

Shaping lines and curves is more involved than shaping ellipses or rectangles because:

▼ Lines and curves have multiple nodes.

▼ Each node has at least one control point (but may have several).

There are three different types of nodes.

1. **Smooth nodes** have two control points and always lie on a straight line. Whenever you move one control point, the other one moves to maintain through the node the smoothness of the line.

2. **Symmetrical nodes** have all of the qualities of smooth nodes, but the two control points are always equidistant from the node. As a result, the curvature on both sides of symmetrical nodes is always the same.

3. **Cusp nodes** and their control points are not necessarily in a straight line. Therefore, you can move each control point independently, which, in effect, controls either of the segments meeting at the node. Use a cusped node when you want to make a sharp change of direction or point between two segments.

A segment can be either a line segment or a curve segment.

▼ A **line segment** uses a straight line to connect two nodes. There are no control points associated with a straight line

▼ A **curve segment** has control points associated .with it, one for each side of the node.

Now that we understand some of the terminology, let's begin shaping some curves.

1. Draw an S-shaped curve on the page using the Pencil tool.

2. To make it easier to work with, Zoom in on the curve, either by using the zoom in tool, or by using the right-hand mouse button if you programmed it for 2x zoom.

3. Select the Shape tool from the toolbox. When your cursor becomes a black arrowhead cursor, select the node at one end of the curve. If it's still hard to see the node, zoom in on it again.

4. Now that your curve is easy to see, let's investigate what happens when we shape the curve by dragging the node. To move the node that you've selected, drag it anywhere on the screen. When you move the node, you move the position of the node relative to other nodes in the curve. However, the angles of the curve (which are governed by the control points) remain the same.

If you want to move the first node on the curve (designated by the larger node box), press the **Home** key to select it. If you want to move the last node on the curve, press the **End** key.

SHORT CUT

5. You can also shape your curve by dragging a control point. However, doing this shapes the curve in quite another manner. Dragging a control point *does not* change the position of the node relative to other nodes, but it *does* change the angle of the curve as it leaves the node.

Let's summarize how nodes and control points affect the shape of a curve:

▼ A curve always passes through its nodes.

▼ Each node has two control points, except for a node that is at the beginning or ending point of the curve.

▼ The shape of a curve between nodes is determined by the control points of each of the nodes.

▼ The control point determines the angle at which the curve meets the node.

▼ When a control point is further from its node, it creates a greater curvature. Conversely, a control point closer to the node produces a shallower curve.

▼ A control point positioned directly on top of a node has no impact on the direction or shape of the curve.

▼ To create a symmetrical curve, position symmetrically the control points for the adjacent node.

THE NODE EDIT MENU

The Shape tool also contains a node pop-up menu to edit individual nodes, as shown in Figure 6.6. Access this menu by double-clicking on a node or a line segment.

Figure 6.6 *The Node Edit menu.*

Before we show you the node edit option, let's look at our S-curve with its nodes.

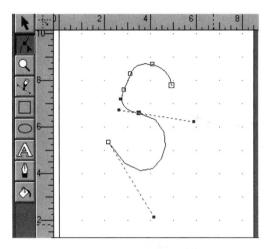

Figure 6.7 *An S-curve and its nodes.*

ADDING NODES

You may want to add another node to a curve. This gives you more control over shaping the curve. Double-click on a node, or a point on a segment exactly where you want to add a node. When the pop-up menu appears, select **Add**. A new node is displayed where you double-clicked on the node or segment. Now you can use the new node and its control points to shape your curve.

You can also add nodes between several nodes. First, select the segments or nodes adjacent to the segments where you want to add the nodes. Either select each one while holding the **Shift** key or use the marquee-select method. To marquee-select several nodes, click and drag the mouse over the nodes you want to include. Release the mouse button.

You can also use these two methods to select multiple objects whenever you are working with the Pick or Shape tools.

N O T E

DELETING NODES

You may also want to delete nodes along your curve to create a smoother shape. It is common to get unwanted extra nodes caused by extra movements you made with your mouse when you created the curve. To delete a node, double-click on the node or the line segment following the node you want to delete, and select **Delete** from the Node pop-up menu. CorelDRAW deletes the node and redraws the curve.

You can press the **Del** key to delete selected nodes.

SHORT CUT

You can select and delete several nodes or segments at one time using one of the multiple select methods in conjunction with Delete from the menu or the **Del** key.

N O T E

JOINING NODES

With the pop-up menu, you can also join two end nodes together, closing an open path.

1. Select the nodes you want to join, either by using marquee-select or by holding the **Shift** key while you select each of them.

2. Double-click on one of the selected nodes.

3. Select **Join** from the pop-up menu.

The two end nodes are joined, and the curve is recreated as a closed path.

You can also join the end nodes from two separate paths to create one continuous path. First, however, you must make them part of the same object.

1. Select both objects.

2. Choose **Combine** from the Arrange menu.

Although the objects look the same, they now function as one object. The status line reflects this—it reads *Curve* instead of *2 objects selected*.

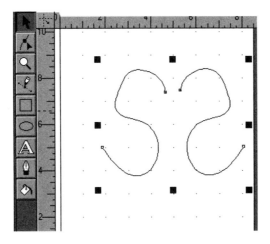

Figure 6.8 *Combining two objects.*

3. Switch to the Shape tool, and marquee-select the two end nodes that you want to join.

4. Double-click on one of the selected nodes, and choose **Join** from the pop-up menu. The curve is drawn as a single path.

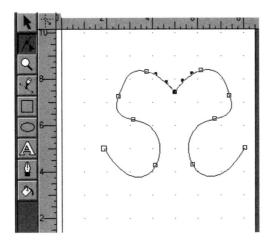

Figure 6.9 *Joining end nodes from two objects.*

BREAKING CURVES

You can also use the Node Edit pop-up menu to break a curve at a single node.

1. Double-click at the node or the spot along a segment where you want to break the curve.

2. Select **Break** from the pop-up menu. The curve is broken at that point and two nodes appear, superimposed upon each other.

Once you've broken a closed path it becomes an open path and you can not fill it.

NOTE

You can also break a curve at several points simultaneously by selecting all of the locations (nodes) where you want to break the curve. Double-click on one of the nodes, and select the Break tool. The curve separates at all of those locations.

The Node Edit pop-up menu has an Align option that lets you vertically or horizontally align two nodes to make it easier for two shapes to share the same outline. To align two nodes:

1. Select both nodes.

2. Click on one, and select **Align** from the pop-up menu.

3. When prompted, select **Horizontal** or **Vertical** and click on **OK**. The two nodes are aligned in the manner you specified.

Just as with joining, if the two nodes you wish to align are in separate objects, you'll first need to combine them before they can be aligned.

LINE AND CURVE CONVERSIONS

To Line converts a curve to a straight line.

1. Double-click on the curve segment or its end node with the Shape tool.

2. Select **To Line** from the pop-up menu. The control points disappear and the line segment is transformed into a straight line.

To Curve converts a straight line to a curve.

1. Double-click on the line segment or its node with the Shape tool.

2. Select **To Curve** from the pop-up menu.

3. Two segments appear on the line, indicating that it is a curve (although it still appears straight). You may now reshape the curve.

As with many of the other Node Edit options, you can apply To Curve or To Line to multiple segments.

CHANGING NODE TYPES

The Node Edit pop-up menu also has options that change the type of node to Cusp, Smooth, or Symmetrical.

1. Double-click on the node you want to change.

2. Select the new type from the pop-up menu.

Remember that symmetrical, smooth, and cusped nodes are characterized by the control points of the node.

SUMMARY

This chapter has shown you how to use the Shape tool to:

▼ Add rounded corners to rectangles and squares.

▼ Transform circles and ellipses into arcs and wedges.

▼ Use the Zoom tool to magnify (or reduce) your drawing for ease of viewing.

▼ Shape lines and curves interactively.

▼ Change lines and curves with the Node Edit menu by adding, deleting, joining, or modifying nodes.

ADDING TEXT TO GRAPHICS

Text can take the form of artistic lettering or paragraph text, and you can either create it in CorelDRAW or import it from another word processing application.

This chapter covers:

- ▼ Artistic text.
- ▼ Editing text.
- ▼ Modifying text.
- ▼ Paragraph text.
- ▼ The Text menu.
- ▼ Symbols.

ARTISTIC TEXT

If you plan to create special effects with your text, you'll need to use artistic text. Artistic text is best suited for incorporating small amounts of text into your graphics. Each block of artistic text is limited to 250 characters. if you need to add more text, either begin another string or use paragraph text.

Let's begin with placing text in your graphic:

1. Select the **Text** tool, represented by an A. Figure 7.1 shows the Text tool fly-out menu.

2. Click on the page to position the cursor.

3. Type in your text.

SHORT CUT
Press **F8** to select the Text tool.

Figure 7.1 *The Text tool fly-out menu.*

While you are typing, you can use any of the normal Windows editing keys (including **Backspace** to erase what you've done) to modify your text.

You can also change the contents of a text string directly on the screen by clicking on the text while the Text tool is selected. To erase a portion of the text string, highlight it, then press **Del**.

EDITING TEXT

Once you've entered text, you can change any of its attributes (such as its style or typeface) by selecting the text with the Pick tool, then selecting **Edit Text** from the Edit menu. The Artistic Text dialog box is displayed, as in Figure 7.2.

Press **Ctrl-T** to access the Artistic Text dialog box.

SHORT CUT

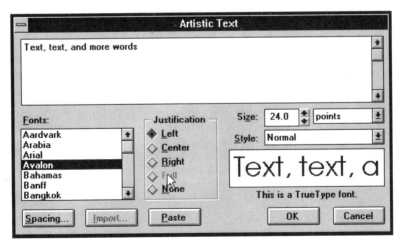

Figure 7.2 *The Artistic Text dialog box.*

The top part of the dialog box contains a text entry box that allows you to enter or edit text. There are scroll arrows that allow you to move up and down in this entry box. While you are in the text entry window, you can use any of the following keys:

▼ **Backspace** deletes the character to the left of the cursor.

▼ **Del** deletes the character to the right of the cursor, or any text that you highlight with your mouse.

▼ **Left/Right Arrows** move your cursor through the text.

▼ **Home** brings your cursor to the beginning of the current line.

▼ **End** brings your cursor to the end of the current line.

▼ **PgUp** brings your cursor to the first line of the current text string or paragraph.

▼ **PgDn** brings your cursor to the last line in the text entry window.

▼ **Enter** begins a new line.

Below this panel is a preview window, showing how the text looks in the font that you have selected. To the left is a list of the fonts available. There are over 150 typefaces included with CorelDRAW. You can also include others that are in compatible formats, or create your own. With most standard typefaces, you can choose normal, italic, bold, or bold-italic styling by clicking on the style names from the drop down list. Figure 7.3 shows some examples of different typefaces.

Not all typefaces have all styles available.

NOTE

Avalon Text

Dawn Castle Text

Toronto Text

Figure 7.3 *Examples of fonts.*

Notice that you can scroll through the list of fonts (and watch the preview box change), to help you make a selection.

Select a point size in the box given, either by scrolling with the arrow, or by entering a value.

Justify your text, left, right, center, full, or none by pressing the appropriate Justification radio buttons.

This is left justification.   This is center justification.   This is right justification.

Figure 7.4 *Examples of text justification.*

Adjust the spacing by clicking in the Spacing box. The Text Spacing dialog box, displayed in Figure 7.5, is displayed. All of the values that you enter in this box will be a percentage of the point size.

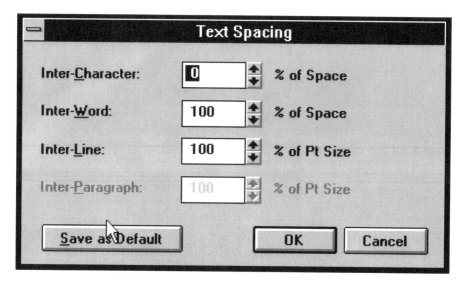

Figure 7.5 *The Text Spacing dialog box.*

Intercharacter spacing determines the space between each character. The default value is 0. If you make the value positive, the spacing between characters increases. If you make the value negative, the spacing decrease. Figure 7.6 shows examples of positive and negative intercharacter spacing.

ThisisO%interwordspacing.

This is 50% interword spacing.

This is 100 % interword spacing.

Figure 7.6 *Examples of intercharacter spacing.*

Interword spacing works in much the same way, except that the default values start at 100, which means that the space between each word is the size of a character. Figure 7.7 shows examples of interword spacing.

ThisisO%interwordspacing.

This is 50 % interword spacing.

Figure 7.7 Interword spacing.

Interline spacing is the space between the baseline of one line to the baseline of the next line. Proper interline spacing keeps the bottoms of the lowest character from touching the top of the highest character on the next line.

Interparagraph spacing is grayed out for artistic text because it is available only for paragraph text.

You can save as defaults the new values you create by clicking on **Save as Default** before you click on **OK**.

The Artistic Text dialog box also allows you to paste text from the Windows clipboard. This is covered in the section on editing paragraph text.

MODIFYING TEXT

You've already used the Pick tool to move, stretch, shrink, rotate, skew, and mirror objects such as rectangles, ellipses, lines, and curves. The Pick tool performs the same operations on your text. Let's start with the sample text shown in Figure 7.8.

Sample text string

Figure 7.8 A sample text string.

With the string selected, click on the Pick tool. Drag the text by one of the corner handles to proportionally scale the text object. Check the status line, and notice that the point size is changed.

You can also stretch or shrink text by dragging on one of the middle handles. The point size changes although the text is not stretched proportionally, as displayed in Figure 7.9.

Sample text string

Figure 7.9 Stretched text.

Double-click on the object to get the double-headed rotating and skewing arrows. Dragging one of the corner handles rotates the object, as shown in Figure 7.10.

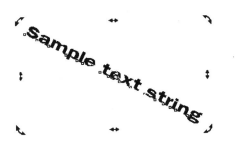

Figure 7.10 *A rotated text object.*

Drag one of the middle handles to skew the object, as displayed in Figure 7.11.

Figure 7.11 *A skewed text object.*

You can also create a mirror image of the text by dragging a middle handle either vertically or horizontally through the selected text string, as shown in Figure 7.12.

Figure 7.12 *A mirrored text object.*

Any CorelDRAW action that you can perform on objects such as ellipses, rectangles, lines, and curves can also be performed on text. You can also stretch, shrink, scale, rotate, skew, and mirror objects using numerical values in the Transform menu.

PARAGRAPH TEXT

If you're planning to enter a large block of data, use paragraph text. As many as 4,000 characters fit in a block of paragraph text. However, the number of characters allowed is dependent upon the complexity of the typeface you have chosen.

To enter paragraph text:

1. Select the Text Tool.

2. Position your mouse in a corner of the paragraph text frame to be created, and drag in a diagonal direction. As you drag, a dotted marquee-select frame is displayed as shown in Figure 7.13.

Figure 7.13 *A paragraph text frame.*

3. When the frame is the correct size and shape to enclose your text, release the mouse button. You may revise the frame or bounding box for your paragraph text if needed.

4. Type directly into the frame that you've just created. CorelDRAW detects your right-hand margin and wraps your words to the next line.

5. If your frame is not large enough to hold all of the text that you entered, it is not displayed on the screen, as you can see in Figure 7.14.

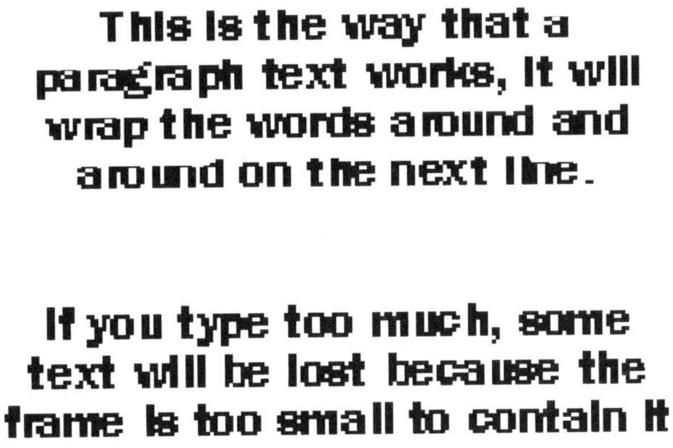

This is the way that a paragraph text works, it will wrap the words around and around on the next line.

If you type too much, some text will be lost because the frame is too small to contain it

Figure 7.14 "Lost" *paragraph text.*

Click on the paragraph with the Pick tool and stretch the paragraph text boundary box larger. The rest of your text appears, as shown in Figure 7.15.

Figure 7.15 *"Found" paragraph text.*

All of the same operations can be performed on paragraph text as on artistic text. However, if you skew paragraph text, only the frame is skewed. The text remains vertical, as displayed in Figure 7.16.

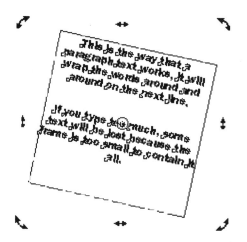

Figure 7.16 *A skewed paragraph text frame.*

You can also select the paragraph with the Pick tool and choose the Edit Text option from the Edit menu (or press **Ctrl-T**) to access the Paragraph Text dialog box shown in Figure 7.17.

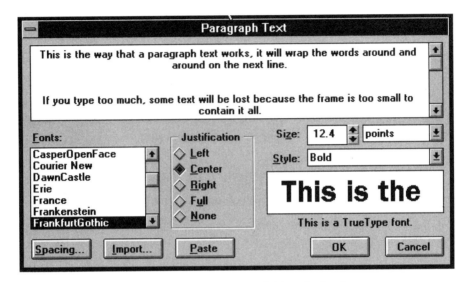

Figure 7.17 *The Paragraph Text dialog box.*

This dialog box looks almost exactly the same as the one for artistic text. It has some additional options. Under Justification, the Full radio button is now accessible. Full justification aligns the text to both sides of the frame, leaving no ragged margins.

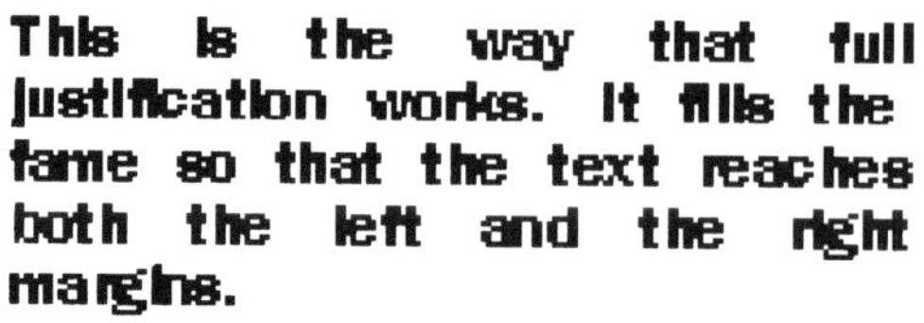

This is the way that full justification works. It fills the fame so that the text reaches both the left and the right margins.

Figure 7.18 Full justification of text.

When you select **Spacing**, the Interparagraph option is now available. This option starts as 100 percent of point size as spacing between paragraph. Increasing the value increases the spacing between paragraphs, decreasing the value reduces the spacing.

There are two other methods of bringing text into CorelDRAW. You can either paste text (which you can use for both artistic and paragraph text) or you can import text, which works with paragraph text only.

PASTING TEXT

Before you can paste text, it must be cut or copied into the Windows Clipboard either from another text box in CorelDRAW or from any other windows package that is compatible with the Clipboard. Cut (**Shift-Del**) removes text and puts it on the Clipboard. Copy (**Ctrl-Ins**) copies the string on to the Clipboard.

To paste text into CorelDRAW, select **Paste** from the edit text dialog box or press **Shift-Insert** and any text from the clipboard is pasted into the dialog box. You must already have something entered in your text string, regardless of whether you are working with artistic or paragraph text. If necessary, enter just one character into the string. As soon as you've imported the Clipboard text, you can delete this extraneous starting character. Any characters over the 4,000 character limit are truncated.

The pasted text has all of the currently selected attributes, such as typeface, size, justification, and spacing. Figure 7.19 shows the Windows Clipboard and the pasted text.

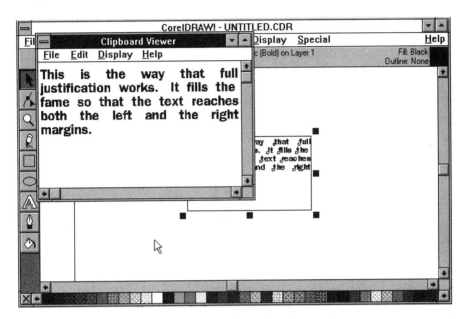

Figure 7.19 *The Clipboard and pasted text.*

IMPORTING TEXT

Another way to bring text into CorelDRAW is to import it. You can only use the import option for paragraph text. You must already have created a paragraph frame, and have at least one character entered in it. From the Paragraph Text dialog box, select **Import**, and the Import Text dialog box is displayed.

Under File Name, you'll see that the filename extension *.TXT is specified. Scroll through the List Files of Type box to see other types of files that you can import.

You can only import files that are saved in ASCII or generic format. Most word processors have the capability of saving files this way. To import files correctly, avoid including tabs and indents in the original file.

If you do not see the file you want in the drive and directory listed, change the drive by scrolling through the drive box and clicking on the directory that contains your file. Select the file you wish to import and click on **OK**. The text is displayed in the text entry box window.

Once you have imported your text, you can edit it either on the screen or in the text entry window.

THE TEXT MENU

Once you've got text on the screen, you can manipulate the string or the paragraph using features in the Text menu.

THE TEXT ROLL-UP MENU

The first item in the text menu is the Text roll-up menu, shown in Figure 7.20.

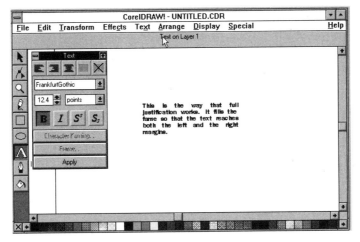

Figure 7.20 *The Text roll-up window.*

You can roll the window up out of your way using the up arrow in the right hand corner and restore it using the –. It may also be moved around the screen to make viewing the document easier.
NOTE

Options in the text roll-up window include:

▼ Change the text justification using one of the five buttons at the top of the roll-up window.

▼ The next box shows the currently selected typeface. To select a different font, click on the drop down arrow, and select one from the list shown.

▼ Increase or decrease the point size by clicking on the up or down scroll arrow, or changing the point size value.

▼ Character kerning or text frame options are available. These options are covered later.

▼ Selecting one of the character icons below the Point Size box, changes the style of your text. Click on the icon showing bold, italic, subscript, or superscript, click **Apply**, and the style of your text changes. Not all styles are available with all typefaces.

CHANGING CHARACTER ATTRIBUTES

You can change the attributes of any character or characters you've selected with the Shape tool or highlighted with your cursor.

Look at the text string shown in Figure 7.21. If, for example, you wish to enlarge only the letter X in this string and make it bold, select the Shape Tool then click on the letter X in text.

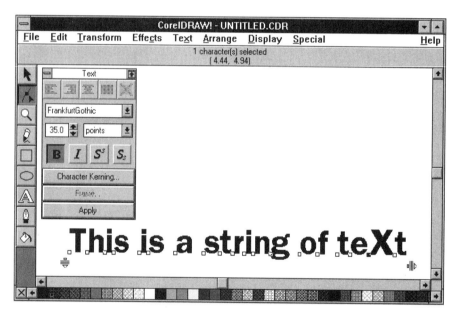

Figure 7.21 *A text string.*

From either the Text menu or the Text roll-up window, double-click on the *X* character. The dialog box shown in Figure 7.22 is displayed.

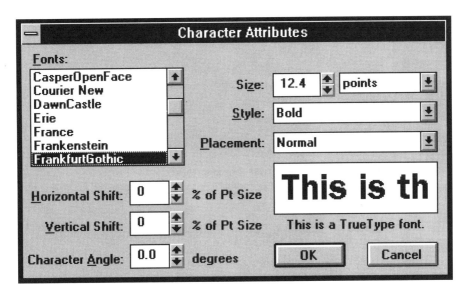

Figure 7.22 *The Character Attributes dialog box.*

You may now set the typeface style, placement, angle, and shift of the selected character(s).

CONTROLLING A PARAGRAPH TEXT FRAME

Select **Frame** from the Text menu (or the Text roll-up window) to access the Frame Attributes dialog box, as shown in Figure 7.23.

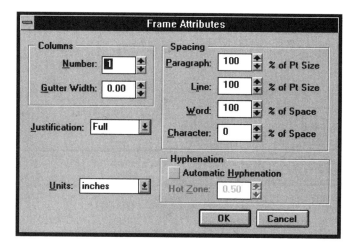

Figure 7.23 *The Frame Attributes dialog box.*

This dialog box controls some of the same spacing selection items accessed through the Text Spacing dialog box. You can also have CorelDRAW arrange your text in columns. Specify the number of columns you want and the amount of spacing you'll need between the columns (gutter width). Your text is reformatted when you click on **OK**.

FITTING TEXT TO A PATH

Interesting and attractive effects are created when you fit text to a path. You can format text around ellipses, rectangles, or curves, as shown in the example in Figure 7.24.

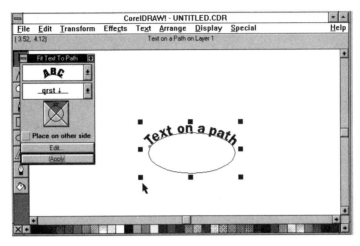

Figure 7.24 *Text fitted to an ellipse.*

To fit text to a path:

1. Create both the text and the path to which you want it fitted, as shown in Figure 7.25.

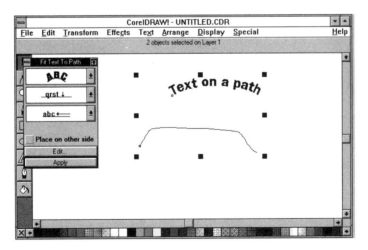

Figure 7.25 *Text and a curve.*

2. Select the path and the text, then select **Fit Text To Path** from the Text menu.

3. The Fit Text To Path roll-up window is displayed. Select the variables you need and click on **Apply**.

4. The text is fitted around the path, as displayed in Figure 7.26.

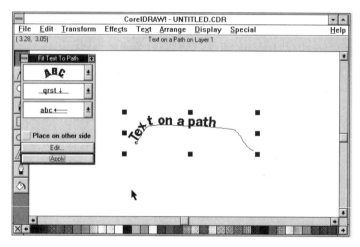

Figure 7.26 *The Fit Text To Path roll-up window and text fitted to a path.*

The best way to work with the roll-up window is to make your selections from all three drop down menus before you apply them. Then, take a look at how the text appears fitted on the path. If you don't like its appearance, you can go back and revise the selections.

You may also decide to change the shape of the path. If you wish to change the path, select the path and its attached text, then select **Separate** from the Arrange menu and modify the path. After you modify the path, you can refit the text to the new path.

If you modify the text, the new text string is fitted to the path.

The path shown in these illustrations was drawn from left to right. However, if your path is drawn from right to left, the text wraps differently around the path. Figure 7.27 shows what happens.

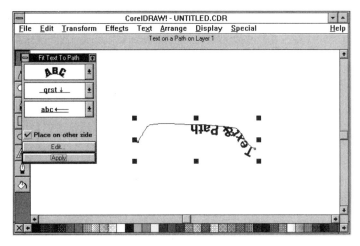

Figure 7.27 *Text on a right-to-left path.*

After you've placed your text on the path, you might want to remove the path. With the text on path selected, choose **Separate** from the Arrange menu, select the path, then delete it. The text is still fitted to the now invisible path.

Let's look at the options in the text roll-up window, and see how they affect the results when you fit your text to a path.

CHARACTERS ROTATED TO PATH BASELINE

The first drop-down menu in the roll-up window selects how the text sits on a path. The options are visually represented, so you can easily choose which one fits your needs.

▼ Rotating letters makes the letters in the text string follow the contours of the path. CorelDRAW may skew some of the letters in the text string both horizontally and vertically, as shown in Figure 7.28, to match the curvature of the path.

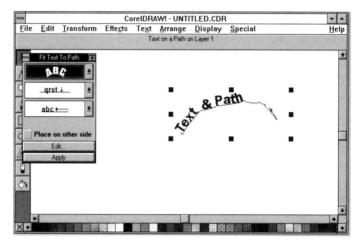

Figure 7.28 *Text fitted with horizontal and vertical skew.*

▼ To skew the letters vertically to fit the path, as shown in Figure 7.29, choose the second option in the drop-down menu. The degree of skew is proportional to the slope of the path.

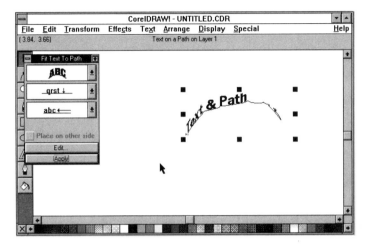

Figure 7.29 *Text fitted with vertical skew.*

▼ To skew the letters horizontally only, as shown in Figure 7.30, choose the third option in the drop-down menu. Again, the slope of the path determines the degree of skew.

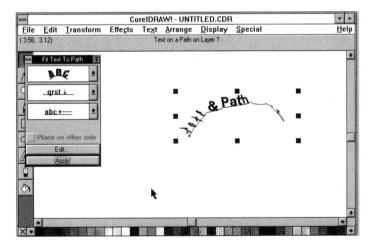

Figure 7.30 *Text fitted with horizontal skew.*

▼ The fourth option maintains the letters in their upright position, regardless of the curvature of the path.

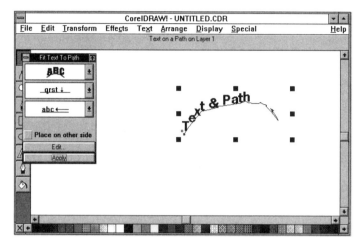

Figure 7.31 *Text fitted with no skew.*

Let's look at a close-up of our first example, showing text skewed both horizontally and vertically, as displayed in Figure 7.32. The baseline of each letter is moved to fit the slope of the path upon which it is placed.

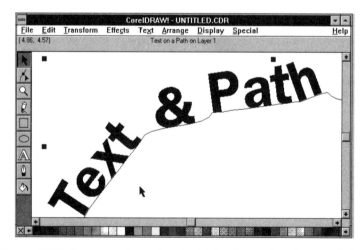

Figure 7.32 *Close-up of text fitted with horizontal and vertical skew.*

TEXT AND PATH DISTANCE

The second drop-down menu in the Fit Text To Path roll-up window specifies the distance of the text from the path. Again, the drop down menu shows all of the options visually.

▼ The first option of the second drop down menu places the text string directly on the path baseline, as displayed in Figure 7.33.

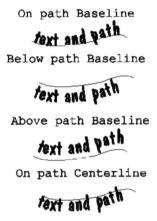

Figure 7.33 *On the path, below the path, above the path, and on the center of the path.*

▼ You can also place the string below the path, but not touching the path.

▼ To place the text above the path without touching the path, select the third option. CorelDRAW calculates how far from the path the text sits.

▼ The fourth option places the text on the centerline of the path, as displayed in Figure 7.34.

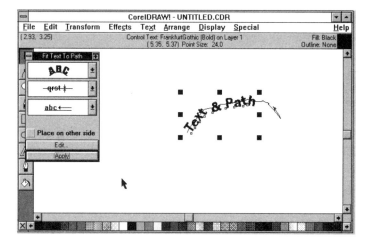

Figure 7.34 *Text placed on a path centerline.*

▼ You can determine how far above or below the path text appears. Click on the fifth option to move the text the desired distance from the path.

You can also specify an exact distance, in inches, that the text sits above or below the path. Click **Edit** in the Fit Text To Path roll-up window. In the Dist From Path field, shown in Figure 7.35 enter a positive value for distance above the path, or a negative value for distance below the path.

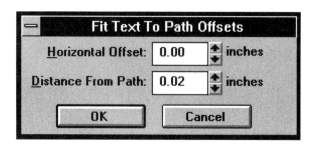

Figure 7.35 *Fit Text To Path Offsets dialog box.*

TEXT PATH ALIGNMENT

The third drop-down menu in the Fit Text To Path roll-up window adjusts the text's alignment to the path.

Alignment behaves differently depending on the type of path you are using. For paths that are not true ellipses or rectangles, but including all other closed paths, there are three possibilities.

▼ By default the text is placed at the starting node of the path, as shown in Figure 7.36.

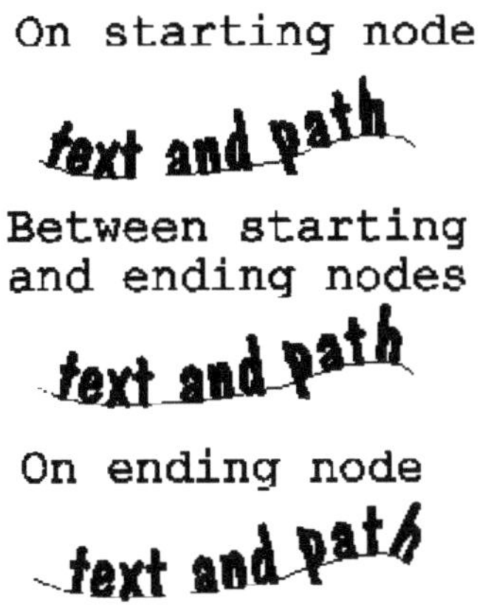

On starting node

text and path

Between starting
and ending nodes

text and path

On ending node

text and path

Figure 7.36 *Text placed on a path's staring node.*

▼ You can also center your text on the path, which positions the text midway between the starting and ending nodes of the path.

▼ The third alignment option fits the text to the last node of the path.

For true ellipse and rectangle objects, (those drawn with the ellipse and rectangle) the path alignment drop-down menu is replaced with an square icon containing a circle, which is divided into four sections. Click on the section in which you want the string to appear, and the text appears in that portion of the rectangle or ellipse. Figure 7.37 shows the text fitted to a quadrant of the ellipse.

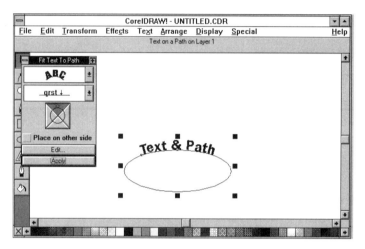

Figure 7.37 *Text placed on top of an ellipse.*

You can also specify the distance that the text is offset from the starting point of the curve. Click on **Edit** in the Fit Text To Path roll-up window. In the Horizontal Offset field, enter a positive value for distance to the right of the starting point, or a negative value for distance to the left of the starting point.

PLACE ON OTHER SIDE

The last option in the Fit Text To Path roll-up window is Place On Other Side. This checkbox reverses all of the specifications you made. Your string is aligned on the opposite side of the path with the text mirrored, as displayed in Figure 7.38.

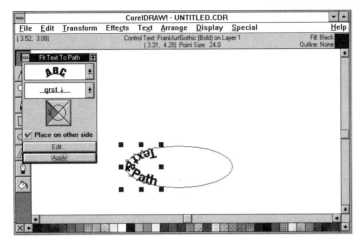

Figure 7.38 *Text fitted to a path, placed on other side.*

OTHER TEXT ADJUSTMENTS

After you have fitted text to a path, you can adjust it by altering either the path or the text. Once you have fitted text to a path, it is interactively linked. Any adjustment you make to the text or path causes the text to be refitted to the path.

To move or kern characters without modifying the path follow these steps:

1. Press the **Ctrl** key and use the Pick tool to select the text that is already fitted to the path.

2. Click on the text and drag the cursor above or below the path. A sliding cursor is displayed. You can use the sliding cursor to move the text any distance from the path. An outline of the path appears when you stop moving the cursor.

3. Drag the text along the path by using the Shape tool, highlighting all of the nodes in the text string, and dragging them to the desired location.

4. You can also adjust the individual character spacing or kerning for the text along the path. Use the Shape tool to move the individual (or a group) of characters along the path.

You may also need to adjust the angles of some of the characters to compensate for their new positions along the path.

This method is fine if you need to change only one or two characters. If you need to adjust several of the characters to achieve a better fit, it may be easier to first return the text string to a straight baseline, make your adjustments, then refit the text to the path. Undo the Fit Text To Path command, make adjustments to the text, then select **Fit Text To Path** again.

There can be no intervening command between Fit Text To Path and Undo.

N O T E

This will often be a repetitive, trial-and-error sequence, until you are satisfied with the arrangement. Once you are approaching perfection and need to adjust the spacing on only a few characters, use the Shape tool to kern your characters.

To start over, you can also use the Straighten Text option, as illustrated in Figure 7.39. Select the text by holding the **Ctrl** key while you click on the text string, then select **Straighten Text** from the Text menu.

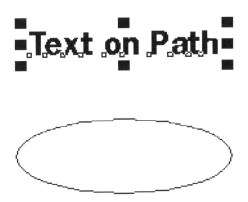

Figure 7.39 *Straightened text.*

This readjusts characters you've rotated or shifted after you fitted the text to the path. All of your original spacing will be lost.

Another way of retracing your steps is to use Align to Baseline, as shown in Figure 7.40. Select the text by holding the **Ctrl** key while you click on the text string. Then select **Align To Baseline Text** from the Text menu.

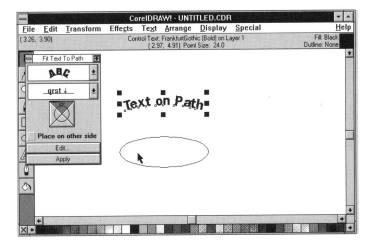

Figure 7.40 *Text aligned to a baseline.*

This resets any vertical shift you've applied to your characters, but does not affect any horizontal shift. This can give you some interesting results.

Any rotation you've done on your characters will be lost.

KERNING

To interactively work with an individual character within a text string, select the string with the Shape tool. Notice that nodes appear next to each letter. In addition to these nodes, spacing control handles are displayed at each end of the last line of artistic text.

To help you interactively kern text, you may wish to zoom in on the string you're working with. Your spacing will be much more accurate if you work with a close-up of your text, as shown in Figure 7.41

Figure 7.41 *Zoomed-in text with nodes.*

If you have selected paragraph text, the spacing control handles appear at the bottom of the text frame.

To move a character, select its node and drag it to a new position. You can also use the arrow keys on your keyboard to move the character. If you hold down the arrow key, the character repeats, that is, moves in continuous small steps for as long as you hold down the key.

You can also work with several characters at once by using either the marquee-select or pressing the **Shift** key while you click.

If you are working with paragraph text, use the marquee-select or the Shift-and-click method to select characters, and move the text to a new location.

SPELLING CHECKER AND THESAURUS

Besides its artistic attributes, you want the text in your graphics to be accurate. There are two options on the Text menu, Spelling Checker and Thesaurus, to help you.

SPELLING CHECKER

To check the spelling of either a single word or a block of text, select the text, then select **Spelling Checker** from the Text menu.

You can select text in one of two ways.

1. To check only a few words in a string, select the Text Tool, then use the mouse to highlight the words you need to check.
2. To check an entire string of artistic or paragraph text, you can select with the Pick Tool.

Then, select **Spelling Checker** from the Text menu, and the dialog box shown in Figure 7.42 is displayed.

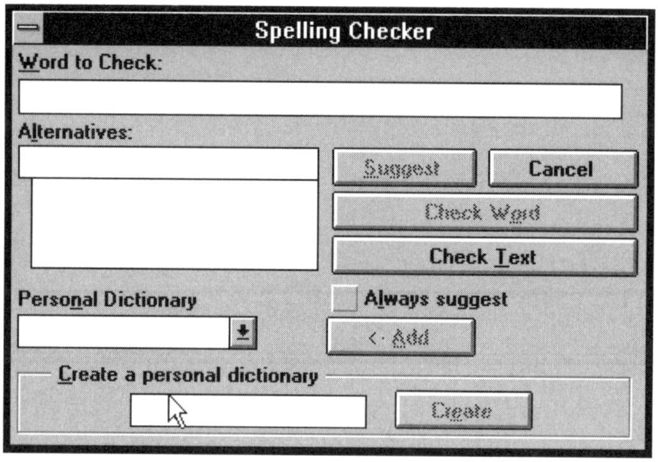

Figure 7.42 *Spelling Checker dialog box.*

Click on **Check Text** and the Spelling Checker begins checking the selected words. If the words are found in the dictionary, the message

Spelling check finished. No spelling errors found.

is displayed. Click on **OK** to return to your normal screen.

If the word is not in the dictionary, the word appears in the Word Not Found field, as shown in Figure 7.43.

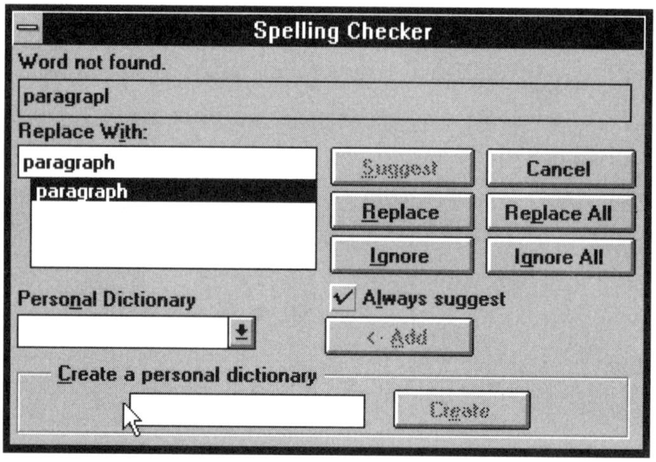

Figure 7.43 *The Spelling Checker dialog box displaying an incorrect word.*

If there are several unrecognizable words in the string that you're checking, the spelling checker presents the next sequential word as soon as you've taken action on the current word.

When a word is not found, you have several options:

▼ **Ignore.** You do not want to replace the word. The next unrecognized word is displayed.

▼ **Ignore All.** The spelling checker ignores this word and all later occurrences of the word. The next unrecognized word is displayed.

▼ **Suggest.** The spelling checker suggests any possible substitutions in the box shown below the Replace With box. If you see the correct replacement, select the word and click on **Replace**. The spelling checker replaces it in the text.

If you click on the Always Suggest check box, the spelling checker always suggest alternate spellings.

If the spelling checker cannot suggest an alternative, or does not present the right alternative for you, you can enter the correction in the Replace With box and click on **Replace** to replace the word in your text. If you want to replace all occurrences of the misspelled word in your text, click on **Replace All**.

The spelling checker *does not* check your replacement word.

Although the spelling checker's dictionary is quite large (it is a Houghton-Mifflin dictionary containing approximately 116,000 words), you may need to create your own supplemental dictionary. This may be especially helpful if you are working in a specialized field, or if you use a great many acronyms, abbreviations, or foreign words. To create a personal dictionary, enter a file name for the dictionary in the Create a Personal Dictionary box and click **Create**. Click on the **Add** button to add the word to your personal dictionary. You may have multiple personal dictionaries for different purposes.

When the spelling checker is finished, it displays a message indicating that it has checked all of the words and returns you to your CorelDRAW screen.

If you wish to exit the spelling checker before it is finished checking the entire text string, click **Cancel**. All replacements that the spelling checker has already made remain in effect.

If you wish to cancel the replacements as well, select **Undo** from the Edit menu. You can also use the spelling checker to verify a word (or suggest alternatives) before you've entered it into a text string. Select **Spelling Checker** from the Text menu with no text selected. When the dialog box appears, enter the word in the Word To Check box and click on **Check Word**. The spelling checker works in the same way as it would with a text string selected.

THESAURUS

Use the Thesaurus to suggest alternate words, or synonyms, for overused words.

With the Text tool selected, highlight a word in a text string, then click on **Thesaurus** in the Text menu. The Thesaurus dialog box is displayed, as shown in Figure 7.44.

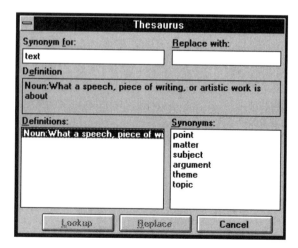

Figure 7.44 *Thesaurus dialog box.*

The word that you highlighted is displayed in the Synonym for box.

You can also use the Thesaurus with no word highlighted. Enter the word that you want to look up in the Synonym field, and click **Lookup**.

If the word is found in the Thesaurus, its definitions and synonyms are displayed in the two boxes below. Click on the alternate that you need, then click Replace. The word is replaced with its synonym in the text.

To close the Thesaurus, click on the **Cancel** button. This *does not* reverse any replacements you have made.

EXTRACT AND MERGE BACK

Although you can spell check and use the Thesaurus on your text, there may be times when you want to edit your text with a word processor. CorelDRAW allows you to extract the text from your file and creates an ASCII file on disk. You can then use your word processor to edit the data, and, provided you've resaved it in ASCII format, merge it back into your CorelDRAW file. The merged text has all of the attributes you originally gave it (typeface, point size, and alignment) as well as transformations such as rotate and skew.

The Blend and Extrude options, covered later, as well as Fit Text to Path, cannot be applied to the remerged text.

N O T E

There are a few simple rules and steps for extracting and merging text.

1. Make sure that the file is exactly as you want it (and saved on disk that way) before you extract your text data. Figure 7.45 shows a graphic including text. If the file is changed, CorelDRAW may have trouble merging the text back into the file.

Figure 7.45 *A graphic with text.*

2. Select **Extract** from the File menu. The Extract dialog box, shown in Figure 7.46, is displayed, allowing you to name the extract file.

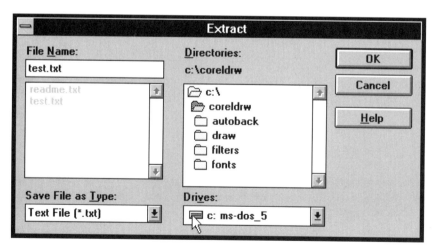

Figure 7.46 *The Extract dialog box.*

3. Close or minimize CorelDRAW. Then, load any word processor and open the extracted file, as shown in Figure 7.47.

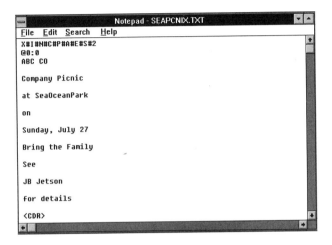

Figure 7.47 *An extracted text file.*

Notice that the file appears as separate, numbered strings. The numbering, as well as the end-of-text marker <CDR> must not be changed. Also notice the order of text string. This sequence must be preserved for CorelDRAW to perform the merge back. Although you're free to add and delete text, remember that it has to fit back into the original file.

4. When you're done editing, save the file as an ASCII text file. If you do not save it as an ASCII file CorelDRAW cannot read it.

5. Open the *.CDR file from which you originally extracted the text.

6. Select **Merge Back** from the Text menu. When the Merge Back dialog box shown in Figure 7.48 is displayed, select the merge file.

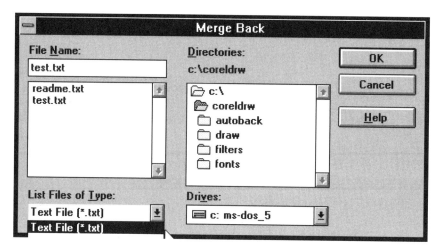

Figure 7.48 The Merge Back dialog box.

Within a few minutes, you'll see the CorelDRAW file, with the revised text merged back in, as illustrated in Figure 7.49.

Figure 7.49 A merged graphic.

SYMBOLS

In addition to all the effects that you can do with text, you may add CorelDRAW symbols to your graphics. The symbols library included with CorelDRAW contains almost 3,000 drawings covering a variety of topics, from buildings to animals, computers, and transportation.

To use the symbols, the symbols library files must have been installed when you installed CorelDRAW. If you find that they were not installed, rerun the installation program and copy only the symbols library to your hard disk.

The text tool works in much the same way as the Pencil tool. If you hold it down while you click, you'll see a fly-out menu. Select the **Star**, and the Symbols dialog box is displayed, as in Figure 7.50.

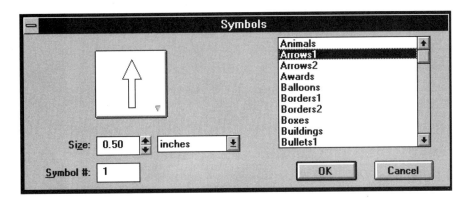

Figure 7.50 *The Symbols dialog box.*

Select the symbol set you want, then click on the sample icon above the size field. A pop-up menu, shown in Figure 7.51, is displayed showing all of the symbols available in that set. Click on a symbol to select it.

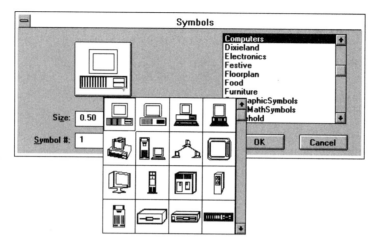

Figure 7.51 *The Symbols dialog box with pop-up menu.*

 You can also look through the CorelDRAW Symbols and Clip
Art catalog to choose the one you want. Note its number, and
N O T E enter its number in the Symbol **#** box.

Specify the symbol size. You can either type the size into the box, or use
the scroll arrows to enlarge or reduce the size value. You can also
change the measurement units by clicking in the units box.

Click on **OK** and the symbol is displayed on the screen. Modify the
symbol just as you would any other curved object in CorelDRAW.

Most symbols are combined objects and must be broken apart for
some editing procedures.

SUMMARY

Text and symbols are objects, and can be modified and manipulated as you would modify or manipulate any other object in CorelDRAW. This chapter has covered many different ways to use text, including:

▼ Placing artistic text in a graphic.

▼ Modifying text.

▼ Creating and editing paragraph text.

▼ Using the Text menu and the Text roll-up menu.

▼ Using the Shape tool with text data.

▼ Adding symbols to your graphics.

MANAGING FILES

This chapter covers the items in the CorelDRAW File menu. Because you put so much work into the drawings that you create, you'll want to save them to work with them again. You may also want to manipulate your drawings in other software packages, or use with CorelDRAW the work that you create in other programs, as well as to print your graphics. This chapter discusses:

▼ Managing files on disk.

▼ Importing files.

▼ Exporting files.

▼ Printing files.

131

MANAGING FILES ON DISK

The New option clears from the CorelDRAW screen whatever you are working on. If you have a drawing on screen that you've modified, CorelDRAW warns you and asks if you want to save the file.

OPENING A FILE

To retrieve a graphics files from the disk, choose the Open option.

SHORT CUT

Press **Ctrl-O** to Open a file.

The Open dialog box, as shown in Figure 8.1, lists all of the files in the current directory. To choose one, click on its name in the File Name list box. However, if the file you want is not in the current directory, you can choose another directory from the directory box.

If you want to see what a file looks like before you open it, click on the filename. If it does not display, click on **Options** to open the rest of the menu, then click on the **Preview** check box. An image of the file is displayed, as shown in Figure 8.1.·

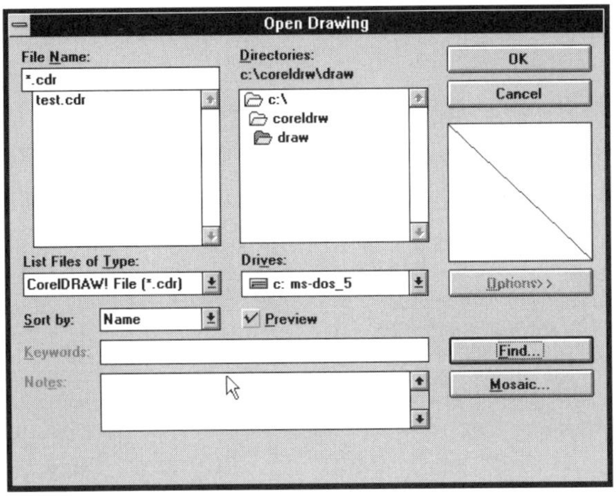

Figure 8.1 *The Open dialog box with preview in effect.*

To make it easier to work with your files, you can sort the file names by name or by date. If you have been assigning descriptive keywords to your files you can also find a file by entering a keyword in the Keyword box and clicking on **Search,** as shown in Figure 8.2. If you're looking for a file, and you're not sure in which directory it is, select **Search All Directories** before you do the search.

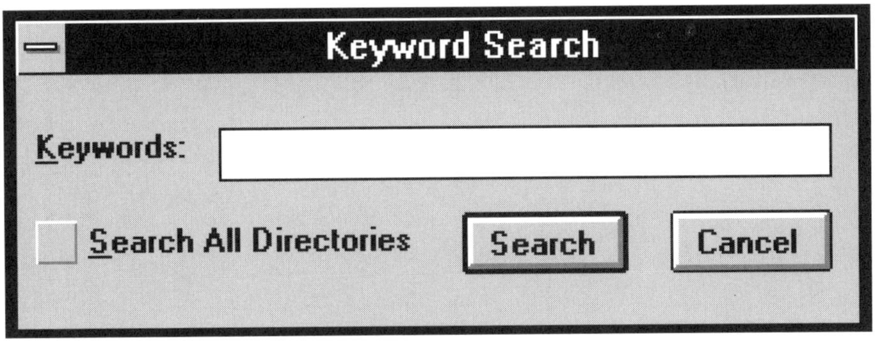

Figure 8.2 *The Keyword Search dialog box.*

SAVING FILES

When you select **Save**, the file is automatically saved, with the name appearing on the title bar on the current directory. All information about the file, including page size and orientation, print selections, and grid and guideline choices, saved with the file.

Press **Ctrl-S** to save the file.

Whenever you save a file, an automatic backup of the file is created with the .BAK filename extension.

To save a file with a new name, choose the **Save As** option. The Save Files dialog box, shown in Figure 8.3 is displayed. Make any changes necessary, including changing the file name or directory in which the file is saved.

If you make extensive changes to a file and still want to retain an original, use Save As and give the new version another name. You can include keywords or notes about the file to make it easier for you to find and retrieve it the next time you want to read the file. You can also specify an Image Header Type, which is a small file with a sketch of your file that allows you to preview the file contents when you want to retrieve it.

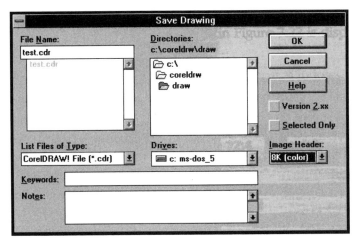

Figure 8.3 *The Save Drawing dialog box.*

IMPORTING FILES

You can import files of many different formats, from a variety of applications, into your CorelDRAW graphics. Refer to the notes in the reference manual for specific considerations for each file format.

CorelDRAW imports the following types of files:

▼ CorelDRAW   *.CDR

▼ CorelTRACE   *.EPS

▼ CorelPhotoPAINT   *.PCC

▼ Windows Bitmap   *.BMP

▼ Windows Metafile   *.WMF

▼ AutoCAD DXF   *.DXF

▼ CompuServe Bitmap   *.GIF

▼ Computer Graphics   *.CGM

▼ GEM files   *.GEM

▼ HP Plotter HPGL   *.PLT

▼ IBM PIF   *.PIF

▼ Illustrator 88 3.0   *.AI *.EPS

▼ Lotus PIC   *.PIC

▼ Mac PICT   *.PCT

▼ TARGA Bitmap   *.TGA

▼ Tiff 5.0 Bitmap   *.TIF

▼ Text files   *.TXT

To import a file:

1. Select **Import** from the file menu.

2. When the Import dialog box appears, as shown in Figure 8.4, scroll through the List Files of Type selections, and choose the file type you wish to import.

3. A list of files with that extension is listed under File Name. If you don't see the file that you want, be certain if you are pointing to the correct drive and directory. If not, change the drive by clicking on the Drives arrow and selecting a drive from the drop-down menu displayed. Double-click on the directory name to select it.

4. When you see the file you need, either double-click on the filename, or click on it once and then click on **OK**. The file is imported, and is displayed on your screen.

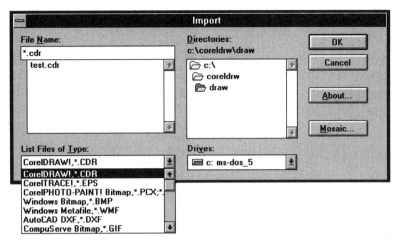

Figure 8.4 *The import dialog box.*

You can also import .TXT files while you are working in paragraph mode. The Edit menu also lets you import text using the Windows Clipboard.

Finally, you can import CorelDRAW clip art files from the clip art directories if you've installed them on your hard drive. Clip art directories contain graphics from a wide selection of graphics companies. Once you've imported clip art into your drawing, you can use them as is, or modify them to suit your own needs. Clip art files are stored in *.CDR format. Clip art is covered further in the section on Mosaic.

Another way to insert "foreign" objects into your graphic is to import an *OLE (object linking and embedding)* object.

1. Select **Insert Object** from the File menu.

2. From the Insert Object dialog box shown, select the application used to create the object you wish to insert.

3. Create or insert the object into your CorelDRAW file.

EXPORTING FILES

You may often use CorelDRAW graphics in other applications. For example, you may want to embed a logo in your word processor file. CorelDRAW exports to the formats:

▼ CorelPhotoPAINT	*.PCC
▼ Windows Bitmap	*.BMP
▼ Windows Metafile	*.WMF
▼ AutoCAD DXF	*.DXF
▼ CompuServe Bitmap	*.GIF
▼ Computer Graphics	*.CGM
▼ Encapsulated Postscript	*.GEM
▼ GEM files	*.EPS
▼ HP Plotter HPGL	*.PLT
▼ IBM PIF	*.PIF
▼ Illustrator 88 3.0	*.AI *.EPS
▼ Mac PICT	*.PCT
▼ Matrix Imapro SCODL	*.SCD
▼ TARGA Bitmap	*.TGA
▼ Tiff 5.0 Bitmap	*.TIF
▼ WordPerfect Graphic	*.WPG
▼ Adobe Type 1 Font	*.PFB
▼ True Type Font	*.TIF

When you select **Export** from the File menu, the Export dialog box is displayed on the screen as shown in Figure 8.5.

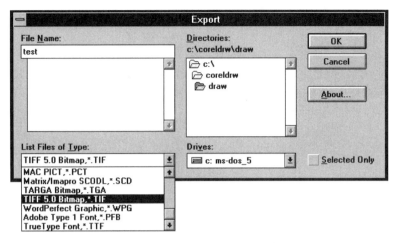

Figure 8.5 *The Export dialog box.*

The options in this dialog box operate in the same way as they do for Import. An additional feature, however, is the ability to export only selected objects by clicking in the checkbox. To do so, you must select the objects that you want to export *before* you choose **Export** from the File menu.

There are special considerations when exporting each type of file. For example, if you are exporting to encapsulated PostScript (*.EPS) format, you'll see the Export EPS dialog box, which lets you select whether all fonts are resident, convert color bitmaps to grayscale, and specify an image header (and select its resolution).

If you export a bitmap image file, you'll see the Bitmap Export dialog box. This allows you to select the colors, size, resolution, and compression of the exported image.

PRINTING FILES

There are several options and dialog boxes used to print from CorelDRAW. This may look like a complicated process, but for the most part, once you establish your print options, they become the default.

To print a file, select **Print** from the File menu. If you have a dot matrix or laser printer active, the Print Options dialog box, shown in Figure 8.6, is displayed. Postscript printer owners see a much more extensive print menu.

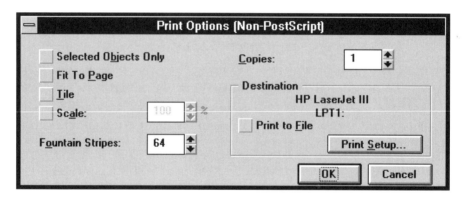

Figure 8.6 *The Print Options dialog box.*

SPECIFYING PRINT OPTIONS

To print only certain objects, select the objects before selecting Print. Then click on the **Selected Objects Only** checkbox in the print dialog box.

You can also specify the number of copies you want to print. Either type the number of copies you want, or click on the scroll arrows to increase or decrease the number. Some basic printers don't allow you to set the number of copies—they print one at a time.

It doesn't take twice as long to print two copies as it does to print one. The greatest amount of time is to process your drawing for the printer. Therefore, if you think you'll need multiple copies, print them all at once.

It takes time to process a CorelDRAW graphic for print, so be patient. Now may be a good time to take a short break. Of course, the more complex the drawing, the longer it will take. To speed up your printing, you may want to lower the print resolution while you are printing drafts of your graphic, and print it at high resolution only when you are ready for your final copy.

Other print options include:

▼ **Fit To Page** fits your graphic to the currently selected page size. This allows you to print larger graphics to a smaller size paper.

▼ **Tile** prints an oversized drawing on several pages, if necessary.

▼ **Scale** stretches or shrinks your graphic and also allows you to print a large graphic on a smaller page.

▼ **Print To File** processes your drawing for print and writes it to a disk file. When you select Print To File, you'll see the dialog box shown in Figure 8.7. Your disc may now be moved to another computer and spied to the printer. As with the Save As dialog box, you'll have the opportunity to change the file name or the drive and directory on which the print file is written. Print files are saved with a .PRN file extension.

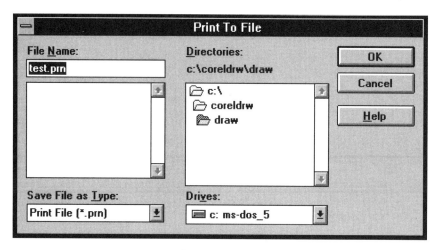

Figure 8.7 *The Print To File dialog box.*

If you have a PostScript printer, you'll see a different dialog box.

If you have difficulty printing a file it may be because you are printing many complex objects that could cause errors in your PostScript printer. It might be a good idea to simplify your curves by reducing the number of segments included in them. The normal curve flatness setting is 1. Increase it to simplify, or flatten, the curves. If you click on the **Auto Increase** checkbox, CorelDRAW automatically increases the curve flatness. This either prints the object, or if it still too complex, causes the printer to skip the object and print the rest of the file.

For a PostScript printer, the Fountain Stripes option lets you choose the number of stripes that the printer uses to create a fountain fill. A higher number of fountain stripes shows a smoother transition between the different shades but prints more slowly. A lower number results in more visible color bands and faster printing times. You may need to experiment to get an optimum setting.

Reducing the Fountain Stripes setting speeds up your print times while you are printing drafts of your objects. Later, you can increase the number when you're ready for the final copy.

A PostScript printer also lets you create color separations. This prints your image on several pages, with different colors on each. To activate this option, click on **Print As Separations** and set your options from the Color Separations dialog box.

If you choose **Print As Separations**, the Crop Marks & Crosshairs, Film Negative, and Print File Info options are automatically selected.

▼ **Film Negative** prints the file as a negative (for an imagesetter).

▼ **Crop Marks & Crosshairs** shows the marks delineating the edges of your drawing and the color registration for the print in the printout. To see these marks, the printable page must be smaller than the physical page.

▼ **Print File Info** prints the filename, the current date and time, and the color information outside the left-hand margin of your page. As with the Crop Marks & Crosshairs option, however, the printable page must be smaller than the physical page for this information to actually print.

Click on the **Within Page** checkbox to print the information inside the left-hand margin of your page.

▼ **All Fonts Resident** assumes that your graphic uses only the fonts resident in your PostScript printer.

▼ **Print Options** (PostScript) dialog box to sets the screen frequency. The default options are determined by the currently selected printer.

PRINT MERGE

Let's get back to the File menu. The next item is Print Merge, which lets you replace text in a drawing with text from a word processor. This works a lot like Extract and Merge Back in the Text menu. The advantage to this feature is that your merged texts take on the characteristics (such as typeface, point size, spacing, and justification) of the text you created with CorelDRAW but you can easily produce multiple personalized copies. For example, you could create a certificate, as shown in Figure 8.8, and customize it with individualized text.

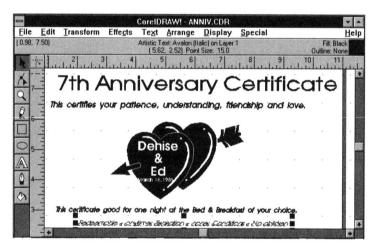

Figure 8.8 *An anniversary certificate.*

The text that you merge with your CorelDRAW files must have the following characteristics:

1. The text must be in an ASCII file, with the filename extension .TXT. Most word processors save files in ASCII format.

2. The first line of your merge file must indicate the text string to be replaced, which must appear exactly the same way (including any capitalization) as it does in your CorelDRAW graphic, as displayed in Figure 8.9.

Figure 8.9 *An anniversary certificate with generic names.*

This is called a *primary text string,* and is entered in your word processor.

3. In your merge file, each primary text string must be preceded and followed by a backslash (\).

4. Follow each *primary text string* by the corresponding *secondary text strings* (the data that will be inserted). These must be in the same sequence as the primary text string, and must also be preceded and followed by a backslash. The primary and secondary text strings are shown in Figure 8.10.

.\Name1\\Name2\\Monthember, dd, yyyy

.\Debbie\\Clifford\\Feb. 14, 2000

Figure 8.10 *A merge file with primary and secondary text strings.*

 Although you may insert as much text as you want, be aware of the space that you have allowed in the CorelDRAW graphic to make sure that it fits.

Once your merge file is ready, select **Print Merge** from the file menu, and click on the merge text filename in the dialog box, as shown in Figure 8.11.

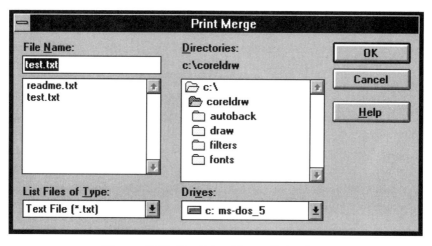

Figure 8.11 *The Print Merge dialog box.*

This dialog box works in much the same way as the Open dialog box, which enables you to select files.

Once you have chosen your merge file, CorelDRAW automatically displays the appropriate Print Options dialog box to allow you to finish setting up your printout. The final result is displayed in Figure 8.12.

Figure 8.12 *The certificate with merged names.*

PRINT SETUP

Choose the Print Setup dialog box to select one of the installed printers. Either keep the default, or use the scroll arrows to select a specific printer. If, you need to choose a different printer, click on **Options**. You can also use the Print Setup dialog box, shown in Figure 8.13, to determine whether the page is printed with portrait (vertical) or landscape (horizontal) orientation, and to specify the paper size.

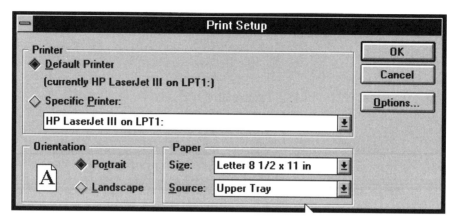

Figure 8.13 The Print Setup dialog box.

PAGE SETUP

Page setup is typically used to print to the same size and orientation of paper you used when you created your drawing. You may want to use the Page Setup options, displayed in the dialog box shown in Figure 8.14, when you initially start your graphic.

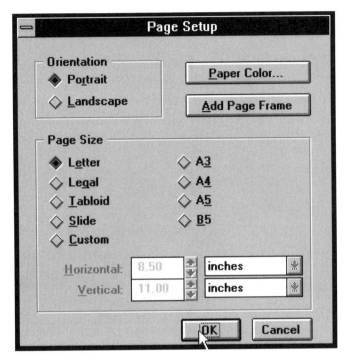

Figure 8.14 *The Page Setup dialog box.*

In addition to the portrait and landscape choices you'll also want to set the size of your page. Choose one of the standard page sizes listed, or select Custom, then set the measurements and units of measurement for the page size.

To get a peek at what your printout looks like if it will be printed on colored paper, set the Paper Color, using the dialog box shown in Figure 8.15. This colors the editing window to match your selection.

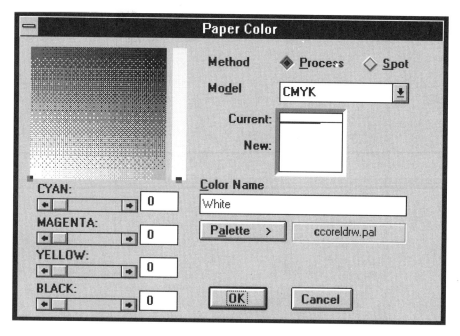

Figure 8.15 *The Paper Color dialog box.*

Another option is Add Page Frame, which creates a printable frame for a or background for your drawing.

At the bottom of the File menu, as shown in Figure 8.16, you'll see the names and paths of the last four CorelDRAW (*.CDR) files with which you have worked.

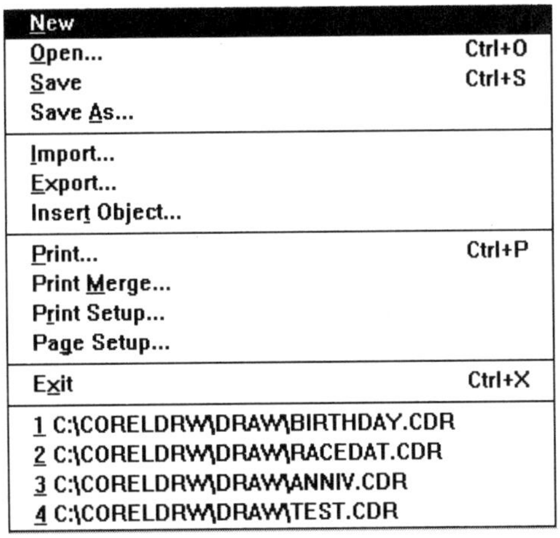

```
New
Open...                                    Ctrl+O
Save                                       Ctrl+S
Save As...

Import...
Export...
Insert Object...

Print...                                   Ctrl+P
Print Merge...
Print Setup...
Page Setup...

Exit                                       Ctrl+X

1 C:\CORELDRW\DRAW\BIRTHDAY.CDR
2 C:\CORELDRW\DRAW\RACEDAT.CDR
3 C:\CORELDRW\DRAW\ANNIV.CDR
4 C:\CORELDRW\DRAW\TEST.CDR
```

Figure 8.16 The File menu with the names of the four most recent .CDR files.

SUMMARY

The File menu has some very powerful features to manage your CorelDRAW files on disk, use files from other applications in CorelDRAW, write your CorelDRAW files on disk in other formats so that you can use them in other applications, and to print your graphics so that you can enjoy the fruits of your labors. We've covered several options to help you manage your graphics files, including:

▼ Opening CorelDRAW files.

▼ Saving your CorelDRAW files on disk, and attaching keyword information to make subsequent retrieval easier.

▼ Importing files in formats other than CorelDRAW into your graphic.

▼ Exporting your CorelDRAW files to other formats, so you can use them with other software.

▼ Printing your CorelDRAW files, including:

- ◆ Specifying print options.
- ◆ Selecting a printer.
- ◆ Using the Print Merge feature.
- ◆ Designating the page setup.

ARRANGING OBJECTS

When you are working with CorelDRAW, your drawing is not just a result of the objects that you put into your graphic and their coordinate positions, but their positions relative to each other. You can place objects in front of or behind other objects, align several objects together in a variety of positions, group or ungroup two or more objects, or you can combine several objects into one curve and later break them apart.

This chapter covers:

▼ Aligning objects.

▼ Changing an object's position.

▼ Grouping objects.

▼ Combining objects.

▼ Separating objects and converting objects to curves.

▼ Layers.

ALIGNING OBJECTS

You may want to align your objects, that is, line them up in a certain direction. Even though you could do that by carefully placing them with your mouse according to your rulers and your grid, CorelDRAW provides for a much easier method. Look at the flowchart symbols in Figure 9.1, and see how you can align the different elements.

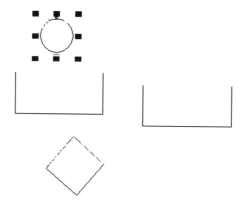

Figure 9.1 *Drawing of flowchart symbols.*

The objects don't quite line up, but we can fix that.

1. Use the Pick tool to select the objects that you want to align.

2. Choose the circle at the top, and the rectangle directly under it.

3. Select **Align** from the Arrange menu. The Align dialog box, shown in Figure 9.2, is displayed.

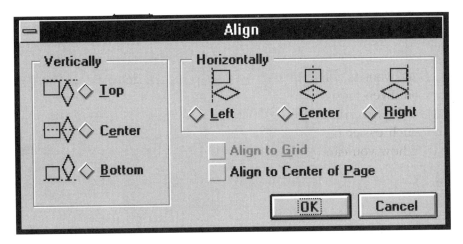

Figure 9.2 The Align dialog box.

4. Look at the diagrams shown with the radio buttons. If you want the circle centered over the rectangle, select **Center** from the Horizontal section. Click on **OK** and the two objects line up correctly, as displayed in Figure 9.3.

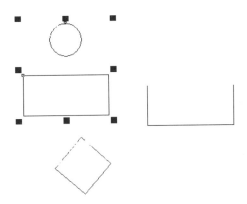

Figure 9.3 Aligned circle and rectangle.

5. Now look at the diamond-shaped decision box, and the rectangle just to the right of it. To align them vertically, select **Center** from the Vertical section, and click on **OK**. The two objects line up, as shown in Figure 9.4.

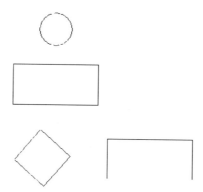

Figure 9.4 *An aligned diamond and rectangle.*

6. You can also align objects in two directions at a time. Choose the diamond and the circle. From the dialog box select **Right** and **Bottom**. Click on **OK**, and the objects are aligned.

If you select your objects using the mouse with the **Shift** key, the last object that you select is the basis of the alignment. All other selected objects are aligned with it. However, if you select your object with the marquee-select, the first object that you created is the basis of the alignment. Unless you have a very good memory and know which object you created first, you may want to select your objects with the Shift method to make your results more predictable.

N O T E   If you select **Align to Grid** or **Align to Center of Page**, the aligned objects are repositioned as a group to the grid or the center of the page, respectively.

Press **Ctrl-A** to select the Align dialog box.

SHORT CUT

CHANGING AN OBJECT'S POSITION

If you've included many objects in your drawing, you'll find that the graphic looks quite different, depending upon which object is in the foreground and which object is in the background. To get an idea of what we're talking about, let's look at a few views of the same objects, in the same relative grid locations on the screen, as shown in Figures 9.5 and 9.6.

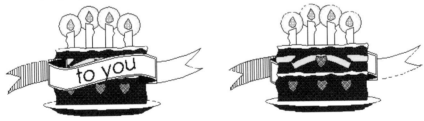

Figures 9.5   *Figure 9.6*
Graphics with different arrangements.

The Arrange menu has several options to help you order your objects. You can place objects in front of or behind others, or you can bring an object to the foreground or background of a graphic. To illustrate many of the options in the Arrange menu, we'll use the row of horses shown in Figure 9.7.

Figure 9.7 *A row of horses.*

If you wish to bring a particular object to the foreground, select it using the Pick tool, and select **To Front**. In the example shown here, selecting the dark horse before choosing To Front places it on top of all of the other horses, as shown in Figure 9.8.

Figure 9.8 *A row of horses with the dark horse in front.*

Press **Shift-Pg-Up** to select the To Front option.

The Arrange menu also places an object in the background. Select it using the Pick tool, then choose **To Back**.

Press **Shift-PgDn** to select To Back.

The Forward One and Back One options are similar to To Front and To Back. However, instead of bringing the selected object on top of (or behind) all the other objects, it simply advances or retreats the object *one* position. Let's look at our row of horses again. Select the fourth horse in line, and see how Forward One works, as displayed in Figure 9.9.

Figure 9.9 *The gray horse placed forward one.*

Press **PgUp** to select Forward One. Press **PgDn** to select Back One.

Finally, you can reverse the order of several selected objects. Select all of the horses, then select **Reverse Order** from the arrange menu. The row of horses is displayed as shown in Figure 9.10.

Figure 9.10 *A row of horses in reverse order.*

GROUPING OBJECTS

You can group several objects together so that you can treat them as one entity. This is very similar to doing a marquee-select or selecting multiple objects using the Shift key. In fact, you'll need to select the several objects that make up your group before you can actually apply the Group command from the Arrange menu.

Once the objects are grouped, you can move, resize, rotate, or skew the group without changing any of the objects' relative position. You can tell by the status line whether you have multiple objects selected. If you have a group of objects selected, the status line reads *Group of 6 objects on layer 1.*

SHORT CUT

Press **Ctrl-G** to Group objects.

N O T E

You can also group together groups of either two or more groups and individual objects using the same technique.

One disadvantage to a group is that you can't edit the individual objects separately. Therefore, you may at some time want to ungroup them.

Select the group, then select **Ungroup** from the Arrange menu. The status line reflects the number of objects selected.

If you have other groups embedded within the group, you may need to ungroup them as well.

N O T E

Press **Ctrl-U** to ungroup the group.

SHORT CUT

COMBINING OBJECTS

Combine and Break Apart are similar to Group and Ungroup. There's one important difference. Combine converts all of the selected objects to a *single curved object,* and the status line reflects the fact that one curve is currently selected.

Select all of the objects you wish to combine, then select **Combine** from the Arrange menu.

Press **Ctrl-C** to combine selected objects.

SHORT CUT

There are several advantages to combining several objects into one:

1. You can edit all of the objects as one entity.
2. You can use the Shape tool to edit several nodes at once in the newly created curve, even though the line segments are not attached.
3. You can conserve memory by combining complex objects.

4. Combing objects can create interesting effects with multiple overlaid objects, such as masking.

To uncombine the object, select it and choose Break Apart. The curve then appears as a series of separate objects, and the number of objects selected are reflected in the status line.

SHORT CUT

Press **Ctrl-K** to engage Break Apart.

SEPARATING OBJECTS AND CONVERTING OBJECTS TO CURVES

Separate breaks apart objects that you created with a blend or separates text that has been fitted to a path.

Convert to Curves converts text, ellipses, and rectangles to curved objects that you can manipulate with the Shape tool. Text may be converted to a graphic using Convert, which allows full editing capability of all Bezier curve nodes and control points.

LAYERS

Another way to superimpose objects on top of each other is to place them on different layers. Generally, only one layer is active at a time, which means that you can only work on one layer with your commands. However, all of the layers are part of your drawing, and you can switch back and forth between layers. You can also make layers invisible (and then make them visible again), or print individual layers rather than the entire graphic.

To manage the different layers in your drawing, use the Layers roll-up menu, shown in Figure 9.11, which is the top item in the Arrange menu.

Figure 9.11 *The Layers roll-up menu.*

Layer 1 is the default layer, which means that unless you create another layer, all of your work appears on Layer 1. To demonstrate how layers work, let's draw a rectangle and a circle on layer 1, as in Figure 9.12.

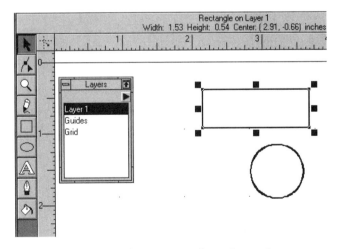

Figure 9.12 *A rectangle on Layer 1.*

The grid and guidelines are on their own separate layers, but they govern your work in all of the layers that you create.

To create a new layer, click on the black right arrowhead and from the menu shown, select **New**. The Layers Option dialog box, displayed in Figure 9.13, appears, allowing you to set the options for this layer.

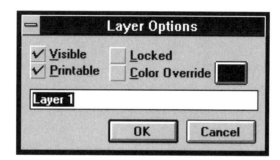

Figure 9.13 *The Layer Options dialog box.*

By default, the layer that you are creating is visible. To make it invisible, click on the checkbox. When you are working on a complex drawing, you may want to put part of it on an invisible layer.

The Printable option is also selected by default, but you can deselect the layer and eliminate it from your printout.

Color Override lets you assign a color to all objects in the layer, but creates the color as a wire frame outline. This may be helpful, especially while you are creating your drawings, because it identifies the objects by layer, yet leaves them transparent, so that you can see all of the objects underneath. If you are working with a great many layers, it's a good idea to assign a separate color to each layer, so that you can easily choose the objects you want.

You can also select the Locked option to prevent you from altering the objects on a layer. You may find this useful if you spent a lot of time and effort creating an object or group of objects, and do not want to alter them by mistake while you're working on other parts of your graphic. Place the complex object on its own locked layer and proceed with your work.

Each new layer is automatically named as the next-higher-numbered layer. However, you're free to choose any name (up to 32 characters) that you want.

Now that you've created Layer 2, let's place an object on it so that we can see how layers behave.

1. Make sure that Layer 2 is active by selecting it in the Layers roll-up menu.

2. Create an ellipse and fill it with gray, so we know where it is. The ellipse on Layer 2 is shown in Figure 9.14. The status line indicates that the currently selected object is an ellipse on Layer 2.

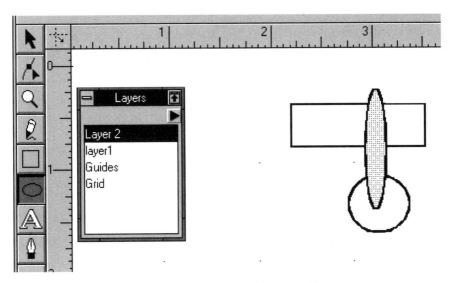

Figure 9.14 *Layer 2 with a gray ellipse.*

3. Since the top-named layer is always the top in the stack of layers, we can expect that the layer 1 objects will be superimposed on top of the shaded ellipse. Press **F9** to preview your graphic, and verify that the layers are ordered correctly.

You can also perform other editing functions with the Layers roll-up menu. When you click on the black right arrow, you can delete the active layer (the layer selected in the roll-up) by choosing Delete.

When you delete a layer, the next layer in the stack becomes the active layer.

You can also use this menu to move or copy an object from one layer to another. Select the object that you want to move or copy. Then, make sure that you select the destination layer in the roll-up window, and click on **Move** or **Copy**. The object is transferred to the new layer.

Copy leaves the object on the original layer, while Move removes it from the original layer.

If you wish to be able to work on all the layers at the same time, click on the Multi-Layer option. You then select any object, regardless of which layer it's on.

You can also change the stacking order of the layers. For example, to make Layer 2 the top layer, click on Layer 2 in the roll-up menu, and while the mouse button is depressed, move Layer 2 up over Layer 1. Notice that Layer 2 is now at the top of the list. If you press **F9** to preview your drawing, you'll see that the objects on Layer 2 are superimposed on the Layer 1 objects.

Let's take a look at this drawing, with a white circle on Layer 1, a gray ellipse on Layer 2, and a black rectangle on Layer 3. Depending on how the layers are stacked, our graphic appears very different, as shown in Figures 9.15, 9.16, and 9.17.

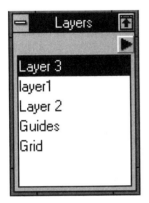 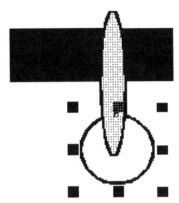

Figure 9.15 *Layer 3 on top.*

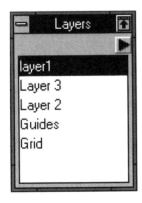 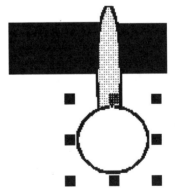

Figure 9.16 *Layer 1 on top.*

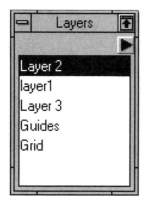
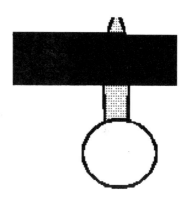

Figure 9.17 Layer 2 on top.

SUMMARY

You can use the objects that you've created to compose many different graphics, and by using the Arrange menu, you have seen how you can make several different drawings from the same object by:

▼ Aligning objects with each other.

▼ Moving objects in front or in back of some or all other objects.

▼ Reversing the order of objects.

▼ Grouping objects to move, scale, or resize them as a single group (and later ungroup the objects if you need to work on each object separately).

▼ Combining several objects into a single curved object to perform node editing (and later break them apart if you wish to treat the objects separately).

▼ Separating objects that have been blended or text fit to a path.

▼ Converting text to curves so that you can apply node editing.

▼ Using layers to dynamically arrange objects, hide objects, make portions of your drawing read-only, or exclude portions of a drawing from printing.

CHAPTER

10

CREATING SPECIAL EFFECTS

Now that you know how to create and modify shapes with CorelDRAW, you'll probably want to learn how to create all of the exciting effects you see in brochures, magazines, and advertisements.

This chapter covers:

▼ Envelopes.

▼ Perspective.

▼ Blending objects.

▼ Extrusion.

There are several choices in the Effects menu, shown in Figure 10.1, to help you.

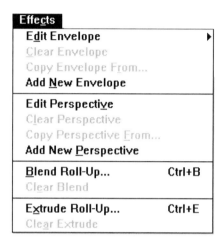

Figure 10.1 *The Effects menu.*

ENVELOPES

The first group of selections on the Effects menu works with envelopes. When you work with an envelope, your object is placed in one of four modes. Pull on any of the handles of your envelope to distort your object in the direction that you choose.

To illustrate how different envelopes work, let's add an envelope to the word *Envelope*.

1. Select the object, and click on **Edit Envelope**. A fly-out menu appears, as displayed in Figure 10.2, that illustrates the four types of editing envelopes available in CorelDRAW: straight line, single arc, two curves, and unconstrained.

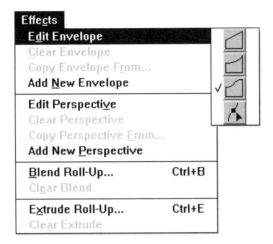

Figure 10.2 *The Edit Envelope fly-out menu.*

2. Select the top item, **Straight Line**. A red editing envelope with eight handles appears around the object, as shown in Figure 10.3.

Figure 10.3 *The editing envelope.*

All initial editing envelopes look the same, regardless of which envelope you've selected.

NOTE

3. Click on the handle that is in the direction that you wish to pull the object. When you release the mouse button, the object takes on the shape of the modified envelope, as shown in Figure 10.4.

Figure 10.4 *A straight-line envelope.*

4. Select **Undo** from the Edit menu to start over.

5. Select **Edit Envelope** from the Effects menu and select the single-arc envelope. When the editing envelope appears, grab the same handle as before, and pull the object. Notice how different the single-arc envelope looks, as shown in Figure 10.5.

Figure 10.5 *A single-arc envelope.*

6. Undo your changes again and select **Edit Envelope**. This time, select two-curves mode and pull the figure to see the effects of the envelope, as displayed in Figure 10.6.

Figure 10.6 *A two-curves envelope.*

You can create many different and interesting effects using the two-curves envelope. You can pull the arcs upward, downward or side-to-side, or even get a twisted effect as shown in Figure 10.7.

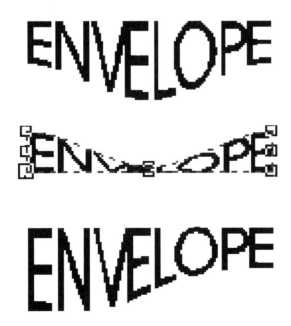

Figures 10.7 *Three examples of using a two-curves envelope.*

If you wish, you can apply an unconstrained envelope. In this mode, you can select more than one of the handles (using either the **Shift** key when you click, or the marquee-select before you click) and pull them. Unlike the first three envelopes, the unconstrained envelope nodes have control points that may be manipulated for further control. This, too, can give some interesting results, as shown in Figure 10.8.

Figure 10.8 *An unconstrained envelope.*

Once you have achieved an envelope style you like, you can copy it to another object. Let's put another text object on the screen, the word *Manila*.

With *Manila* selected, click on **Copy Envelope From** in the Effects menu. An arrow is displayed on your screen. Click on one of the edges of *Envelope* and the same envelope is applied to *Manila,* as displayed in Figure 10.9.

Figure 10.9 The Envelope *envelope copied to* Manila.

To clear the last or only envelope you applied to an object, select **Clear Envelope** from the Effects menu.

Although there are only four types of envelopes, a lot can be done with them. As you go on, you'll see that you can do even more, adding effects upon effects.

PERSPECTIVE

Another special effect that is easy to do with CorelDRAW is to apply mathematical perspective to an object. Rather than viewing an object on a flat plane, you can make one or more of its sides move off in the distance, giving it a feeling of depth.

When you select an object and click on **Edit Perspective** from the Effects menu, you'll see a dashed box (similar to the Envelope box) appear around your object. This box, however, has four small handles. To see how perspective works, put the word *Perspective* on the screen and select the Perspective option, as shown in Figure 10.10.

Figure 10.10 Perspective *in the perspective box.*

1. To show a one-point perspective, move the cursor over one of the handles and drag either horizontally or vertically in the direction you want your object to "vanish."

2. For a two-point perspective, drag diagonally after you have selected one of the perspective handles. Figure 10.11 shows perspective added to an object.

Figure 10.11 Example of perspective.

When you are applying perspectives you'll see an *X* (two, if you're using two-point perspective) on your screen in the distance beyond the receding edge of the object. This is called the *vanishing point*, the point at which a line drawn across the top and bottom would eventually meet. You can see the vanishing point only if it is close enough to be in view.

You can also change the perspective after you've applied it by moving the vanishing point. Dragging it towards the object lessens the perspective. Dragging it away from the object causes more of the object to disappear from view.

Clear Perspective does not remove the perspective if you add an envelope after you put the object in perspective. Conversely, Clear Envelope has no effect if you've since added perspective. NOTE

Just as with the envelope effect, perspective can be copied from one object to another. Put the word *Altered* on the screen, as shown in Figure 10.12.

Figure 10.12 Perspective *in perspective with* Altered *on the screen.*

Select *Altered*, and choose **Copy Perspective From** from the Effects menu. A From arrow is displayed. Move the arrow to the edge of *Perspective* and Click. *Altered* now has the same perspective, as shown in Figure 10.13.

Figure 10.13 Altered *in* Perspective*'s perspective.*

Even after you've put an object in perspective, you can change it. Select your object and select **Edit Perspective** from the Effects menu. CorelDRAW selects the Shape tool and puts the bounding box around the object.

BLENDING OBJECTS

Blending objects makes one object seem to melt into another. As the objects blend, the outline, fill, size, and shape of the first object are transformed to the outline, fill, size, and shape of the second object. CorelDRAW creates all of the shapes or steps along the way, creating a smooth transition from the first object to the second.

To illustrate blending, create two objects, a black rectangle and a white ellipse.

1. With both objects selected, click on **Blend Roll-Up** from the Effects menu. The Blend roll-up window is displayed in Figure 10.14.

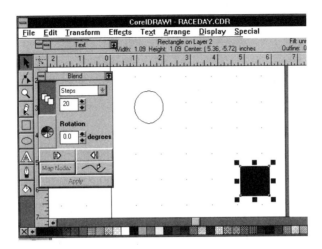

Figure 10.14 *A rectangle and an ellipse with the blend roll-up window.*

2. Using the default values shown, click on **Apply** and the objects are blended, as shown in Figure 10.15.

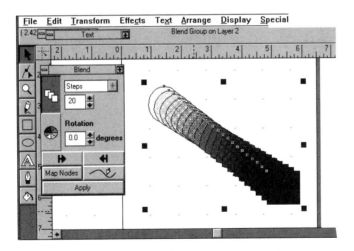

Figure 10.15 *A blended rectangle and ellipse.*

The number of steps specified in this example is 20. This indicates how many intermediate shapes CorelDRAW creates to blend the objects. A greater number of steps creates a more gradual transformation, as displayed in Figure 10.16.

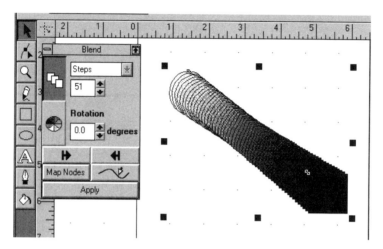

Figure 10.16 *A blended rectangle and ellipse with 51 steps.*

Fewer steps cause a sharper gradation between the two objects.

Fewer steps also result in a greater distance between the blended objects, and more steps yield a smaller distance between the intermediate objects.

You can also change the appearance of your blend by changing the rotation. All of the examples we just looked at showed a 0-degree rotation, which gives you a straight line from point A to point B (or in our case, from the ellipse to the rectangle.) By entering a number in the Rotation box, you can change the slope of the rotation. Watch what happens when you rotate the blend 45 degrees, as shown in Figure 10.17.

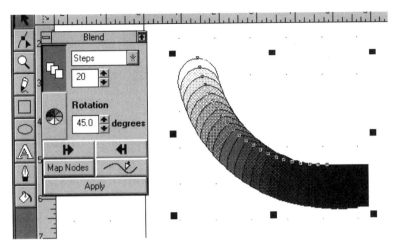

Figure 10.17 *A blend rotated 45 degrees.*

You can also place a blend on a designated path. In this example, we'll create a curved path for the blend, as shown in Figure 10.18.

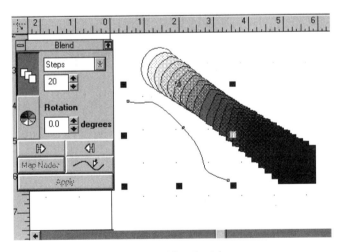

Figure 10.18 *A blend with a curve.*

1. Create the path you want your blend to follow.

2. With the Blend roll-up on the screen, make sure your blend is selected.

3. Click on the picture of the curve in the roll-up menu. Choose **New Path** from the sub-menu.

4. A small hooked arrow is displayed. Place it on the curve, and click.

5. Click on **Apply** and the blend is placed on the curve that you selected, as in Figure 10.19.

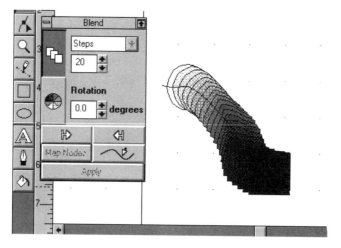

Figure 10.19 *A blend following a Bezier curve.*

Other options on the submenu allow you to show the path of your blend is (by highlighting the path) or remove the blend from its path (Detach from Path).

You can also change the colors in your blend or set the start and end objects in your blend from the Blend roll-up window.

To change the order of the blend, in other words, to place the black rectangle on "top" and the white ellipse on "bottom," select **Reverse Order** from the Arrange menu.

You can also work with individual items within the blend. Make sure that the blend is selected, and select **Separate** from the Arrange menu. A node appears on each of the objects, allowing you to move or shape the individual items.

EXTRUSION

When you extrude an object, CorelDRAW draws in some of the surfaces that illustrate that object's third dimension.

Draw a rectangle and select **Extrude Roll-up** from the Effects menu, as displayed in Figure 10.20.

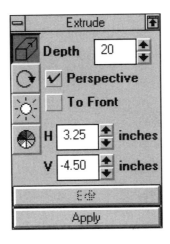

Figure 10.20 *The Extrude roll-up window.*

With the defaults selected, click on **Apply** and the rectangle appears with the extrusion lines shown, as displayed in Figure 10.21.

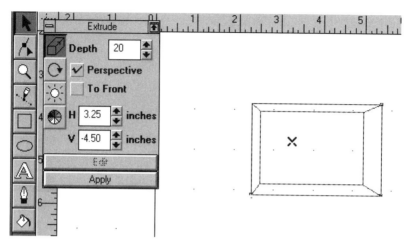

Figure 10.21 *A rectangle with the extrusion applied.*

There is also a Perspective checkbox in the Extrude roll-up menu. If this option is checked, a depth box is displayed, allowing you to specify the depth of the extrusion, as in Figure 10.22.

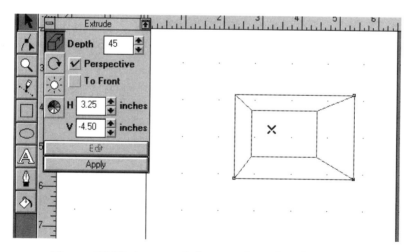

Figure 10.22 *An extruded rectangle with a depth of 50.*

A depth of 99 extends the extrusion all of the way to the vanishing point. A depth of -99 extends the extrusion as far as possible away from the vanishing point.

By clicking on the **To Front** checkbox, the vanishing point is placed behind the object (in other words, the object is in front).

You can also change the location of the vanishing point by changing the horizontal and vertical settings. Horizontal sets the vanishing point across the page. Decrease the value to set it to the left, and increase to move it right. Vertical shifts the vanishing point up (tighter) or down (looser) on the page.

You can apply extrusion to objects that are already in perspective.

NOTE

You can also change the orientation of your extruded object. The second icon on the side of the roll-up menu (the circle with the arrow) is the one that controls spatial orientation. If you click on this option, a three-dimensional sphere appears in the roll-up, with three bands, running horizontally and vertically across the sphere, and around the circumference of the sphere.

If you click on one of the arrows on the horizontal diameter, the object is shifted to the left or right, respectively. Figure 10.23 shows the rectangle with a right orientation.

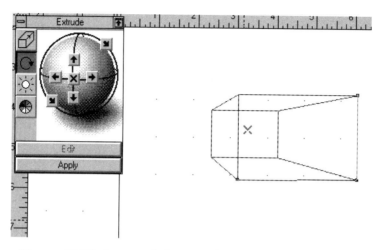

Figure 10.23 *An extruded rectangle with a right orientation.*

Clicking on one of the vertical diameter arrows changes the orientation upward or downward. If you click on one of the arrows around the circumference, the orientation changes in a clockwise or counterclockwise direction.

To add a shaded effect to your extrusion, adjust the hypothetical light source.

1. Choose the sun (the third icon) from the panel on the left side of the roll-up menu.

2. A light switch is displayed in the roll-up menu. Make sure that the switch is On, and a shaded sphere is displayed in the center of a wireframe cube.

3. To locate the light source, click on any point on the wire frame where two lines meet, and click on **Apply**. Figures 10.24 shows the effects of changing the light source.

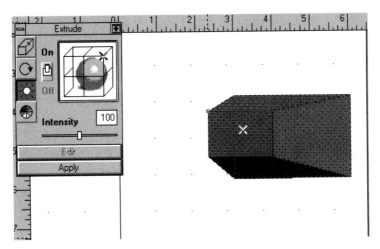

Figures 10.24 *An extruded rectangle with a light source.*

By selecting the color wheel (the fourth icon), you can also change the color of your extrusion.

Although the envelope, perspective, blend, and extrude options give interesting results individually you can combine these options to maximize your effects, as illustrated by the following example.

1. Put the word *Maximize* on the screen, place it in an envelope, and manipulate it.

2. Add perspective, as displayed in Figure 10.25.

Figure 10.25 Maximize *enveloped and put in perspective.*

3. Put the word *Minimize* on the screen. With *Minimized* selected, choose **Copy Envelope From** from the Effects menu, place the arrow on *Maximize*, and click **Envelopes**.

4. Select both *Maximize* and *Minimize*, choose **Blend Roll-Up**, then **Apply**. Figure 10.26 shows the result of the blend.

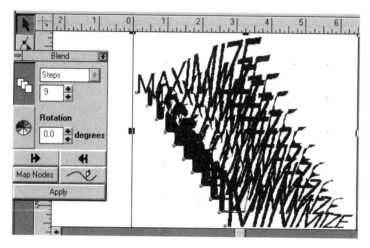

Figure 10.26 *Blended* Maximize *and* Minimize.

SUMMARY

In this chapter, you've learned how to use the options on the Effects menu to add some exciting effects, including.

▼ Shaping an object with different types of envelopes.

▼ Putting an object in perspective to give it a feeling of depth.

▼ Blending several objects along a path and managing the steps in the blend.

▼ Creating three-dimensional effects using extrusion.

MOSAIC

As you work with the different Corel applications, you'll begin to appreciate the difficulty of keeping track of the many graphics files you create.

Mosaic displays a list of all of the files available to you, and also gives you a visual preview of your graphics files. Using Mosaic, you can select a number of files, then perform certain CorelDRAW functions upon them. In addition, Mosaic includes a library function, which compresses your images to conserve your disk space. The Mosaic library allows you to reorganize your graphics, even if they reside in different directories. This chapter covers:

▼ File-management functions.

▼ Select, locate, or find file information.

▼ Libraries.

When you open Mosaic an almost blank screen area is displayed with three items, File, Edit, and Library, on the menu bar.

FILE-MANAGEMENT FUNCTIONS

To begin working with Mosaic, select the **File** menu, shown in Figure 11.1.

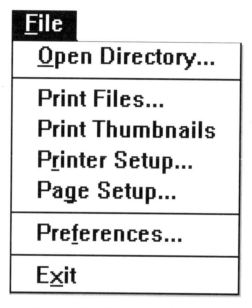

Figure 11.1 *The Mosaic File menu.*

SELECTING A DIRECTORY

Click on **File** and select **Open Directory**. Once you are pointing to the correct drive and directory, select the type of file you want to see from the List Files of Type box. If you click on **Options** you can sort your entries or use keywords to find what you are looking for. Figure 11.2 shows the Open Directories dialog box, with the Options displayed.

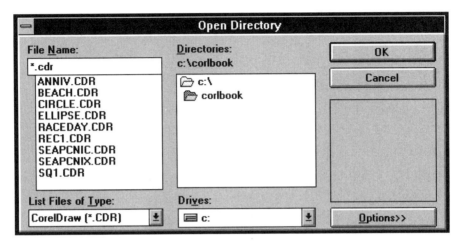

Figure 11.2 *The Open Directories dialog box.*

When you are addressing the directory you need (you'll recognize it by the file names listed), click on **OK** to return to the Mosaic screen. There you'll see thumbnails, small bitmapped representations of your graphics, for all of the files in the selected directory, as illustrated in Figure 11.3.

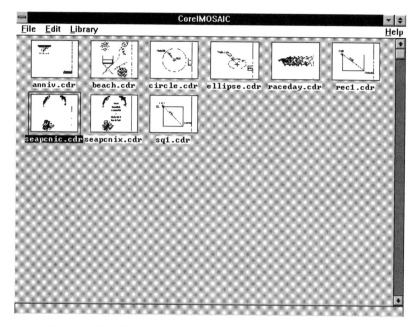

Figure 11.3 *The Mosaic screen with thumbnails displayed.*

DISPLAYING THE THUMBNAILS

To change the way your thumbnails are displayed, click on **Preferences** from the File menu. In the Preferences dialog box, shown in Figure 11.4, choose whether the thumbnails are displayed with Portrait (vertical), Landscape (horizontal), or Square orientation. You can also set the width in pixels. Click on the **Confirm on File Deletion** checkbox, if you want Mosaic to prompt you for confirmation before deleting a file.

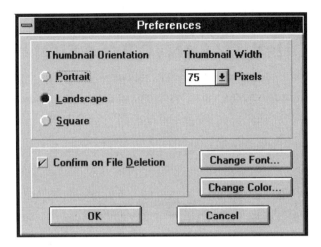

Figure 11.4 *The Preferences dialog box.*

In the Preferences dialog box, you can select the color and font for the thumbnail display, as well as the point size used to name the thumbnails. Click on **Font** to display the Font dialog box.

By selecting **Color** you can change the color used when displaying the thumbnails.

PRINTING FILES AND THUMBNAILS

To print either a file or a thumbnail, click on the file you want. If you want to select more than one file, hold down the **Shift** key while you click on them. If you select multiple files, Mosaic processes the files sequentially, with whatever options you may select, such as Print, Import into CorelDRAW, or Get File Info.

If you select **Print**, Mosaic opens CorelDRAW and the selected files are printed from CorelDRAW. If, however, you select **Print Thumbnails**, the thumbnails are printed from Mosaic. The Printer Setup and Page Setup options in the File menu apply to printing from Mosaic.

SELECTING, LOCATING, OR FINDING FILE INFORMATION

Use the Mosaic Edit menu, displayed in Figure 11.5, to select or deselect files, import and export files to and from CorelDRAW, examine file information, work with keywords, and merge text back into files.

Figure 11.5 *The Edit menu.*

The options in the Edit menu are:

▼ **Select by Keyword** uses keyword information that you previously assigned when you saved the files in CorelDRAW, and selects files based on those keywords.

▼ **Select All** selects all files whose thumbnails appear on the display screen.

▼ **Clear All** deselects any files that are currently selected.

▼ The **Keywords** dialog box, displayed in Figure 11.6, adds or deletes keywords associated with the selected *.CDR file.

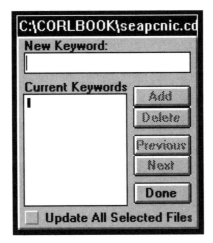

Figure 11.6 The Keywords dialog box.

▼ Use the **Edit** option to open either a *CDR file into CorelDRAW or a *.SHW file into CorelSHOW.

▼ **Import into CorelDRAW** works the same as using the Edit option on a *.CDR file—it opens the CorelDRAW application and brings the drawing onto your screen.

▼ **Export into CorelDRAW** opens the Export dialog box to choose the type of file you want to export.

▼ **Delete** removes the selected file from the specified library or directory. If you checked the **Confirm on File Deletion** checkbox, Mosaic prompts you for confirmation before deleting a file.

▼ **Get File Info** displays the File Information dialog box, shown in Figure 11.7. It includes information about the currently selected file, such as its size in bytes.

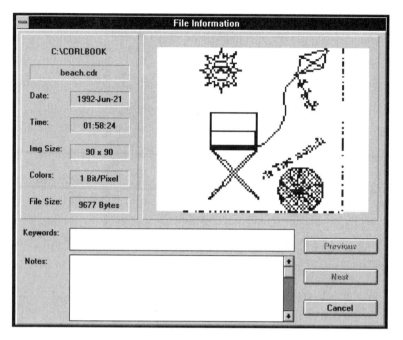

Figure 11.7 The File Information dialog box.

▼ **Extract Text** transfers text from CorelDRAW graphics into ASCII format for subsequent editing.

▼ **Merge Back Into Text** brings a merged text file into CorelDRAW.

LIBRARIES

To compress your files on disk and conserve disk space, you can store your files in a library. Each library consists of two files, a *.CLB file and a *.CLH file. Be sure that both files are present if you move or otherwise manipulate your files on disk. Once you have created the library files, you can delete the original CorelDRAW files from disk.

Test library files by expanding them, and make sure that all of your files are there before you delete the *.CDR files.

N O T E

A library also allows you to reorganize your files in a different way than they are organized in your directories, because your library can consist of files from several different directories.

THE LIBRARY MENU

Use the Library menu, displayed in Figure 11.8, to create, maintain, and expand libraries.

Figure 11.8 *The Library menu.*

OPENING A LIBRARY

To open an existing library, select **Open Library** from the Library menu. The Library dialog box, shown in Figure 11.9, is displayed. From this dialog box, you can select the library that contains the files you need. At that time, the thumbnails of the files in the library are displayed.

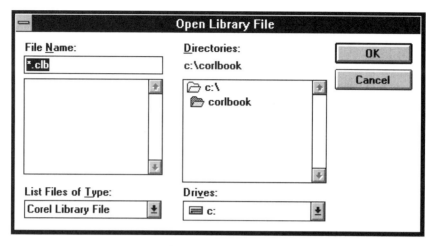

Figure 11.9 The Open Library File dialog box.

EXPANDING LIBRARY FILES

Once your library is selected, you can expand files from the library. Select the files you want and choose **Expand** from the Library menu. The Directory To Extract Files To dialog box, shown in Figure 11.10, is displayed.

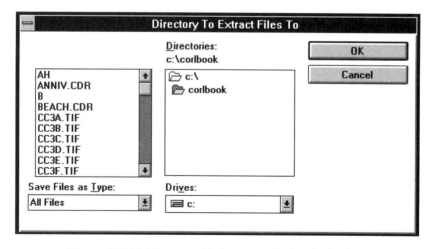

Figure 11.10 Directory To Extract Files To dialog box.

Once the files are expanded, you can choose any other Mosaic option, such as Print or Import, and Mosaic processes the expanded files sequentially.

CorelDRAW cannot open or print a compressed files. You must first expand them with Mosaic.

N O T E

ADDING IMAGES TO A LIBRARY

When you select **Add Images to Library** from the Library menu, Mosaic compresses the selected files and adds them to the library that is currently open.

You can also use **Add Images to Library** to create a new library. Follow these steps:

1. Choose **Select Directory** from the File menu to open the directory that contains the files you want to put into the library.

2. Click on the thumbnails of the files you want to put into your library.

3. Choose **Add Images to Library** from the Library menu and select the directory where you want to locate the new library.

4. Type your new library name into the bar above the File Name box, including the .CLB file extension.

5. Click on **OK**. A confirmation box asks you to verify that the library does not exist and to create the library. When you click on **Yes**, the selected files are added to the new library in the directory that you specified.

DELETING A LIBRARY

When you decide to delete a library, verify that you no longer need the files, or that they are saved in another library or directory. The Delete Library dialog box is shown in Figure 11.11.

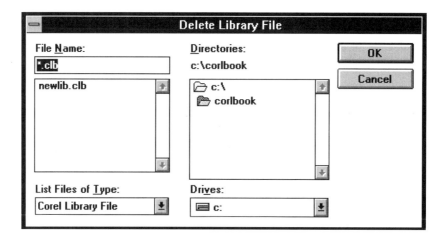

Figure 11.11 *The Delete Library File dialog box.*

Before actually deleting the library, Mosaic displays a confirmation box, asking you to verify the deletion. Click on **Yes** to delete the library.

SUMMARY

In this chapter, you've learned how to use the Mosaic utility to organize your files. To help you find the files you need Mosaic lets you select from a screen full of thumbnails, small representations of your graphics files. Once you select one or more of Mosaic's thumbnails, you can perform a variety of different functions, such as:

▼ Printing files or thumbnails of files.

▼ Importing files into CorelDRAW or CorelSHOW.

▼ Bringing files into CorelDRAW and opening the Export menus.

▼ Selecting files using keywords.

Mosaic also contains a library function, which allows you to compress graphics files and create collections or libraries. To manage your libraries, Mosaic:

▼ Creates libraries.

▼ Compresses files and adds them to a library.

▼ Expands library files.

▼ Deletes libraries.

CORELTRACE

This chapter covers how to use CorelTRACE to edit scanned images and other bitmapped graphics to create better graphics. After you've traced the scanned images, you can use them in other applications, and since they are now vecto-graphics, take advantage of your printer's highest resolutions. This chapter covers:

▼ What CorelTRACE does.

▼ Importing images.

▼ Tracing an image.

▼ Customizing traced images.

▼ The Preferences menu.

▼ CorelTRACE Tips and Tricks.

WHAT CORELTRACE DOES

CorelTRACE traces a variety of bitmapped image types to create vecto-graphics, giving you smooth lines and curves as well as the kind of resolution that takes advantage of high-resolution printers. Tracing your image also produces graphics files that occupy far less disk space than the original images. You can use this program for many different types of images, including technical illustrations, architectural drawings, logos, and letterheads. CorelTRACE replicates colors and shades of gray to give you the closest reproduction of the original.

Once you've traced your image, you can import it into CorelDRAW or CorelPHOTO-PAINT for some additional touch-up work. However, you can also import the traced image directly into other applications, such as Pagemaker, Ventura, WordPerfect, Microsoft Word, Ami Pro, and Arts and Letters.

STARTING CORELTRACE

Begin CorelTRACE the same way you do any of the other applications in the CorelDRAW Program Manager group. Simply double click on its icon, and the main dialog box, shown in Figure 12.1, is displayed.

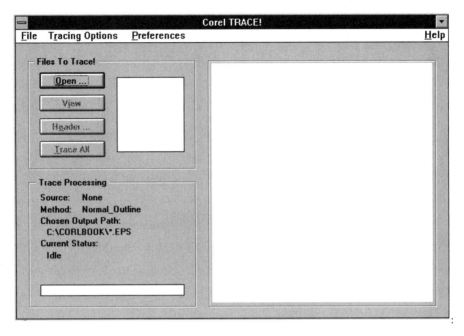

Figure 12.1 *The CorelTRACE main dialog box.*

IMPORTING IMAGES

The acceptable file types for importing image are:

- ▼ TIFF 5.0 bitmaps   *.TIF
- ▼ PC Paintbrush bitmaps   *.PCC, *.PCX
- ▼ Windows bitmaps   *.BMP
- ▼ Compuserve bitmaps   *.GIF
- ▼ Targa bitmaps   *.TGA

In the List Files of Type window, be sure that you are pointing to the type of file that you wish to import. Also, check the drives and directories box to see that you are addressing the drive and directory where your bitmap files are located.

If you click on the **Auto-View** checkbox, you'll see a preview of your bitmap as soon as you select it. The Open dialog box, including the bitmap preview, is shown in Figure 12.2.

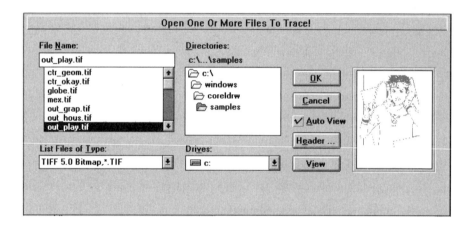

Figure 12.2 *The CorelTRACE Open dialog box with bitmap preview.*

Click on **OK** and CorelTRACE brings your bitmap into CorelTRACE and returns you to the main dialog box.

Before we go on, let's talk a little bit about what makes a good candidate for tracing. High-contrast images make good candidates. Black-and-white line art also traces well. If you'll be tracing color images, those with solid colors trace better than those with shaded color areas. You may also get good results with gray-scale images, which are made up of several shades of gray.

You'll also want to choose artwork that is clear and sharp - so, make sure that you scan it at the highest possible resolution. Fine-tune using the contrast and intensity settings on your scanner to get the best results.

You can use a higher resolution with black-and-white images than with gray-scale or color images. Scanning color and gray-scale images at higher resolutions produces very large disk files without much real improvement in image quality.

NOTE

You may wish to enlarge, or scale, very small images to make them easier to trace. Be careful, however, not to magnify an image more than 300 percent, because that can result in a loss of quality. Conversely, try not to scan overly large images. You can reduce image size by including only the portions you wish to trace, and by cropping unused white space in the image.

TRACING AN IMAGE

Once you've opened an image in CorelTRACE, set your output options and tracing options before beginning the trace.

SETTING OUTPUT OPTIONS

CorelTRACE is unusual because you do not need to do anything to save your traced image.

When you trace the image, it is automatically saved in the designated drive and directory using the same name as the imported image. Therefore, you'll need to set the output options before you the save image. Click on **Output Options** in the File menu. The Output Options dialog box, shown in Figure 12.3, is displayed.

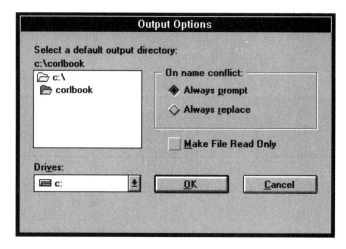

Figure 12.3 *The Output Options dialog box.*

Be sure that you are pointing to the drive and directory where you want to save your traced image files. The On Name Conflict setting wants to know what action you want the program to take if a file by that name already exists. If you select **Always replace**, the program overwrites any old file with the same name on the designated drive and directory—the old file will be lost. If you select **Always prompt**, CorelTRACE warns you that the name already exists. You'll then have the opportunity to overwrite the original file or give the file a new name.

Regardless of which selection you make, you can click on the **Make File Read Only** checkbox. This saves the file as *read only*, which means that you cannot make any changes to it.

TRACING OPTIONS

You must also decide how your trace will be done before you actually trace the image you selected. Click on the **Tracing Options** menu, shown in Figure 12.4.

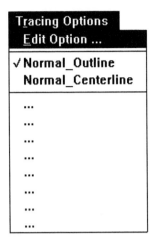

Figure 12.4 *The Tracing Options menu.*

Click on **Normal Outline** to choose the outline method, or **Normal Centerline** to select the centerline method. The blank lines on the part of the menu are used for creating named customized the tracing methods.

OUTLINE

Outline traces the edges of each element, filling in the closed areas of each element with the appropriate color. For example, if you're tracing a black-and-white image, the original colors are preserved in the traced image. For color or gray-scale traced images, CorelTRACE selects the colors that come closest to the original.

Use the outline method for tracing images that consist mostly of thick, filled objects.

CENTERLINE

When tracing with the centerline method, CorelTRACE traces along the center of lines and curves in an object, but not along its outline. Images that are thick and filled are traced like the outline method above. This method works best with images that consist of many thin, black lines.

TRACING

We'll trace the file using the outline method. Click on **Trace All**. The bar at the bottom of your screen shows how much of the tracing process is complete. When it is done, the traced image is displayed on your screen, as illustrated in Figure 12.5.

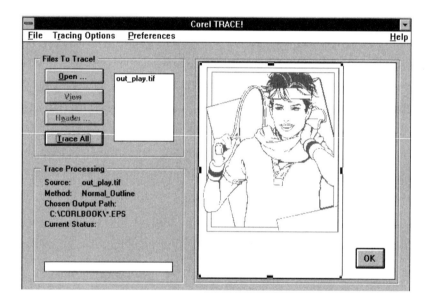

Figure 12.5 *The traced image.*

Now let's look at this traced image in CorelDRAW.

1. Minimize CorelTRACE, then select CorelDRAW from the Program Manager group.

2. Choose **Import** from the File menu.

3. Be sure you are pointing to the drive and directory you selected in the Output Options dialog box. From the List Files of Type box, select *CorelTRACE* *.EPS*.

4. Select the name of the file you just traced and click on **OK**. The traced image is displayed, as illustrated in Figure 12.6. The image had an outline of .028 added to it.

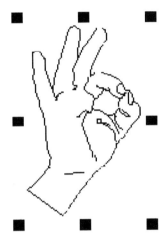

Figure 12.6 *A traced image imported into CorelDRAW.*

Let's go back to CorelTRACE to see how the same image looks when you trace it with the centerline method.

1. Minimize CorelDRAW, then maximize the **CorelTRACE** icon at the bottom of the screen by double-clicking on it.

2. When you're back at the CorelTRACE main dialog box, select **Normal Centerline** from the Tracing Options menu. Open the file.

3. When you return to the main window, select **Trace All**. Because you chose Always Prompt when establishing your Output Options, and you've already saved a traced file with the same name, a warning that the file is about to be overwritten appears.

4. If you click on **No**, the Enter The Trace Destination dialog box, is displayed. Enter a new file name and click on **OK**. The trace proceeds, and the traced file is saved with the new name.

Notice that this imported image has a clearer, crisper outline.

CUSTOMIZING TRACED IMAGES

To customize your traced images, select the **Tracing Options** menu and click on one of the blank lines, shown by the three dots (...). The Tracing Options dialog box, shown in Figure 12.7, is displayed.

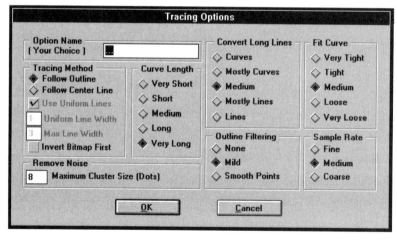

Figure 12.7 The Tracing Options dialog box.

From here, you can make many selections that customize your trace options for tracing specific types of drawings, such as, maps, cartoons, and photographs.

NAMING THE OPTION

The first area in the dialog box is Option Name (Your Choice). Enter the name you want to use to save this set of options. Once you click on **OK**, the options are saved, and the name appears in the Tracing Options menu the next time you select that menu.

If you'll be tracing several different types of images, you can establish and save multiple sets of tracing options. Just be sure to select the one that's appropriate for your image before you begin tracing.

You can always change the options by selecting **Edit Options** from the Tracing Options menu. If you wish to delete the tracing options, simply replace its name with the three dots (...) in the Tracing Options menu.

Let's take a look at how the tracing options work.

TRACING OPTIONS

Select either **Follow Outline** or **Follow Center Line** to use the outline method or the centerline method for tracing.

MAX LINE WIDTH

Max Line Width is available only when you use the centerline tracing method. Max Line Width allows you to specify how many layers of pixels (the dots that make up your image) CorelTRACE removes from the image. A higher number produces a smoother line and a lower setting results in a rougher line. Use a lower setting to most closely follow the original drawing.

USE UNIFORM LINES

Use Uniform Lines applies to the centerline method only. Use Uniform Lines is assigns a specific line weight to all lines in your traced image. This option produces a traced image where all lines are the same width.

INVERT BITMAP FIRST

Use Invert Bitmap First on black-and-white images only. Invert Bitmap First reverses all of the colors (changes black to white and white to black).

REMOVE NOISE

Remove Noise causes CorelTRACE to automatically remove any objects in your image that contain less than the specified number of pixels. This option eliminates some of the dirty areas in your image that may make it look cloudy or smudged. This option may also eliminate some of the detail in your traced image.

CURVE LENGTH

Curve Length limits the size of the individual curves in your traced image. Shortening the curve length increases the amount of detail in your traced image. A shorter curve length also produces more nodes, which, in turn, increases the size of your traced image files.

CONVERT LONG LINES

Covert Long Lines determines whether CorelTRACE converts long lines into straight or curved lines. You'll want to choose the type that most closely duplicates the lines in your original drawing. For example, if you're working on engineering drawings that contain mostly straight lines, select straight lines.

OUTLINE FILTERING

Use Outline Filtering to round out, or smooth, some of the sharp edges in your traced image. Choose **None** if you want to faithfully duplicate the original.

SAMPLE RATE AND FIT TO CURVE

Use Sample Rate and Fit to Curve to control how closely the traced image follows the original. For most images, you can select Medium to get an adequate reproduction. However, if you need a truer duplicate, change these settings, keeping in mind that your resulting traced image also produces a larger file.

THE PREFERENCES MENU

The Preferences menu, illustrated in Figure 12.8, allows you to set certain options that govern how CorelTRACE operates.

Figure 12.8 *The Preferences menu.*

You can change these options at any time to suit the particular image that you are tracing.

TRACE PARTIAL AREA

Trace Partial Area traces (and saves) only a portion of your input image. If you don't need the entire image traced, it's a good idea to do this to save disk space.

Clicking on **Trace All** in the main dialog box gives you a selection box with eight handles (much like the box you use with the Pick tool in CorelDRAW). Move the cursor over one of the handles, and drag the box over the part of the image you want to trace. When you're done, click on **OK**. Figure 12.9 shows an image marked for partial tracing.

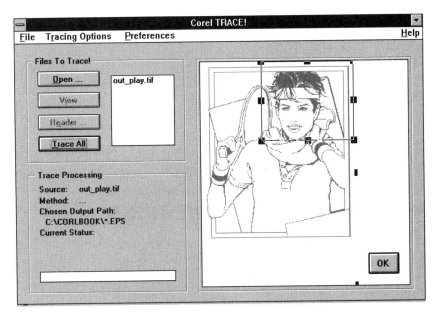

Figure 12.9 *The Partial Tracing selection box.*

PROGRESS RATE AND TRACING INFO

Progress rate and Tracing Info displays an indicator showing what portion of your trace is complete. Current Status tells you the time that is needed to complete the trace, the number of pixels in the image, and the number of nodes and objects in the image. This information is useful for estimating the size and complexity of the traced file. Tracing Progress and Current Status appear in the bottom-left corner of the main dialog box.

VIEW DITHERED COLORS

View Dithered Colors affects only screen display. It determines whether the colors are displayed as dithered or pure.

COLOR REDUCTION

Color Reduction controls the number of colors and shades of gray used to fill the traced image. Choosing a number of colors between four and sixteen results in the clearest traced image. If you're more interested in the shape of the traced image than the colors, select **Convert to Monochrome**.

CORELTRACE TIPS AND TRICKS

Now that we've talked about the CorelTRACE features, let's review some tips and tricks.

- ▼ Because tracing is slow and uses a great deal of memory, move your images from floppy disk to hard disk before beginning your trace.

- ▼ Closing any other Windows applications while you trace leaves more memory available speeding up tracing time.

- ▼ Keep an eye on your disk space, since traced image files tend to be rather large. To help control your file size
    - ◆ Consider tracing in black-and-white, at a lower resolution.
    - ◆ Limit the size of your input images by cropping white space before importing them into CorelTRACE.
    - ◆ Limit the size of your output files by tracing only the portions of the image that you need, and by eliminating unnecessary detail (and therefore, extra nodes) from the output image.

▼ Using CorelTRACE can be very much of a trial and error process. Until you get the feel of it, you may want to experiment with different settings and options to see what the resulting traced image looks like. Remember, too, that you can import the *.EPS file into CorelDRAW, where you can use all of the available tools to add color, modify the outline, and shape the lines and curves.

SUMMARY

This chapter has covered how to use CorelTRACE to trace a variety of image types. You can then import the image into CorelDRAW, where you can examine, and, if you wish, modify, the new file. You've also seen how using the different options can give you control over the traced. You've learned how to:

▼ Import image files into CorelTRACE.

▼ Choose output options.

▼ Select a tracing method.

▼ Trace an image.

▼ Import and work with traced files in CorelDRAW.

▼ Customize your traced images.

▼ Use the Preferences menu.

▼ Work easier and smarter in CorelTRACE.

CORELPHOTO-PAINT

CorelPHOTO-PAINT has several drawing tools you can use to create different effects. This chapter shows you how to use these tools:

▼ The Airbrush tool.

▼ The Spray Can tool.

▼ The Paint Roller tool.

▼ The Paintbrush tool.

▼ The Fountain Pen tool.

▼ The Pencil tool.

▼ The Line tool.

▼ The Curve tool.

▼ The Eraser tool.

▼ The Local Undo tool.

▼ The Color Replacement tool.

▼ The Hollow Box tools.

▼ The Filled Box tools.

▼ The Text tool.

▼ The Eyedropper tool.

▼ The Clone tool.

Before we can begin, open a drawing area. Select **New** from the File menu, and accept the default values from the Create a New Picture dialog box, illustrated in Figure 13.1.

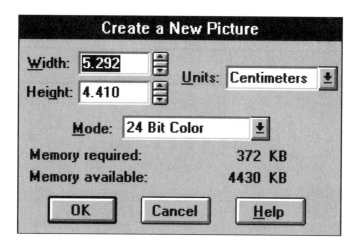

Figure 13.1 The Create a New Picture dialog box.

The first three options that we'll discuss, the Airbrush, the Spray Can and the Paint Roller, are best used to fill large areas of your picture. These selections can be used to create background or shaded effects, or to correct color flaws.

THE AIRBRUSH TOOL

Use the Airbrush tool to do a freehand spray with the primary color. The Airbrush adds shading and depth to your drawing, or corrects flaws.

1. Click on the tool and it becomes available with whatever settings you last had.

2. Choose a primary color from the primary color palette.

Whenever you select a PHOTO-PAINT tool, you always have the option of selecting a new primary, secondary, or background color, or clicking in the Width and Shape workbox to change the width and shape that you will use with that particular tool.

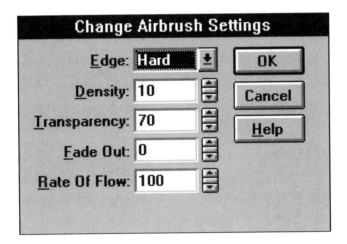

N O T E

3. You can also modify the settings for your airbrush. If you double-click on the tool icon when you select it, the Change Airbrush Settings dialog box is displayed, as in Figure 13.2.

Figure 13.2 The Change Airbrush Settings dialog box.

Using the settings shown, let's do some airbrushing in our picture, and see what kind of effect the airbrush gives. Once the tool is selected, click and drag the mouse over the area that you want to airbrush. A sample of airbrushing is shown in Figure 13.3.

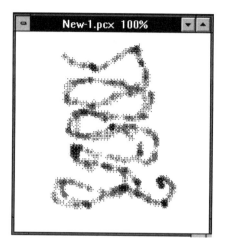

Figure 13.3 *An example of airbrushing.*

If you don't like what you've done, there are several ways to get rid of it.

▼ Select **Undo** from the Edit menu, but remember it only works on the last action you performed.

▼ Press **Alt-Bksp** to undo your last command.

CorelPHOTO-PAINT also has an Erase tool, but this works a little differently. We'll get to it in a while.

THE SPRAY CAN

The Spray Can works like a can of spray paint, and gives you a splattered type of spray. To use the Spray Can, select the tool, then click and drag it over the area you want to spray. Although the result is somewhat similar to the Airbrush, it gives a much rougher effect, as shown in Figure 13.4.

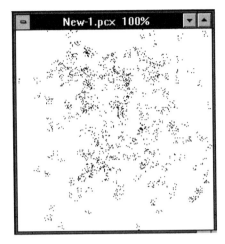

Figure 13.4 *An example using the Spray Can.*

Just as with the airbrush, you can select another primary color, or change the size and shape of the spray can using the Width and Shape workbox.

THE PAINT ROLLER TOOL

The Paint Roller is very handy for filling enclosed areas of your picture. Use it the same way you would to paint your house—when you have large wall areas to do, you'll use the roller, but for tiny areas and trim, you'll want a paintbrush.

An enclosed area can be any part of your picture. For example, if you have a circle or a rectangle, you can fill just that area by placing the small drop inside the shape. On the other hand, if you want to fill your entire picture area, perhaps to create a background effect, you can use the roller. The shape must be fully enclosed or the paint spills out and fills the surrounding area.

Point to the area you want to fill and click the left mouse button. The drop at the end of the roller marks the point where the roller begins to fill the area.

In the corner of the Paint Roller tool you'll notice a small triangle cut-out. This tells you that this is a fly-out tool, which means that you have more than one choice with it.

The paint roller gives you the normal setting, which we've just seen, as well as the gradient and fill pattern paint roller.

THE GRADIENT PAINT ROLLER TOOL

Use the Gradient Paint Roller to fill an area with a shaded color that shades from the secondary to the background color. The Gradient Paint Roller works in much the same way as the Fountain Fill.

1. When you select the Gradient Paint Roller, you can choose several options that affect how your gradient fill appears. First, choose the secondary and background colors, which determines the shaded colors in the gradient.

2. To select which gradient effect you want, click on **Gradient Type** from the Options menu, and from the Select a Gradient Type dialog box, shown in Figure 13.5, select the type of gradient fill that you want.

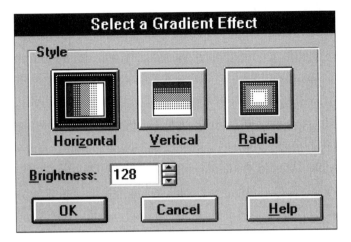

Figure 13.5 *The Select a Gradient Effect dialog box.*

3. When all of your options are set the way you want them, move the roller to the area you want to fill and click the left mouse button. The drop on the gradient paint roller marks the spot where you want the fill to begin. Figure 13.6 shows an example of how a Gradient Paint Roller fills.

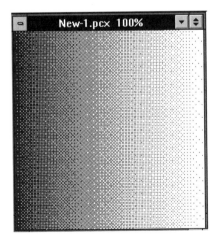

Figure 13.6 *An example of using a Gradient Paint Roller.*

THE TILE PATTERN PAINT ROLLER TOOL

The final paint roller selection is Tile Pattern, which fills the designated area with a repeating pattern, much like wallpaper or floor tile.

Once you have chosen the Tile Pattern Paint Roller, you'll need to select the tile pattern you want to use. CorelPHOTO-PAINT comes with a variety of patterns, or you can create your own.

1. To choose a tile pattern, click on **Tile Pattern** in the Options menu. The Load a Tile Pattern from Disk dialog box, illustrated in Figure 13.7, is displayed.

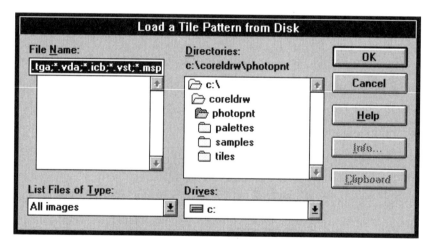

Figure 13.7 *The Load a Tile Pattern from Disk dialog box.*

2. Click on the **Tiles** subdirectory in the CorelPHOTO-PAINT directory.

3. From the list of tile names shown, select the one you want to use.

4. To show you what a tile pattern looks like, we'll select the Southwestern pattern. Point to the area and click the left mouse button. As illustrated in Figure 13.8, the area is now "wallpapered" with a Southwestern pattern.

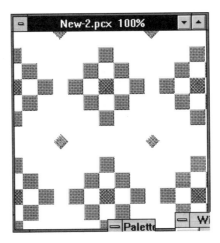

Figure 13.8 *An example of a tile pattern.*

You've just seen how you can fill rather large areas of your picture with the Airbrush, Spray Can, and Paint Roller. Although these options are useful for background work, you can also use them over other objects you've already drawn. When you're ready to do some experimenting, try it and look at some of the results you can get.

THE PAINTBRUSH TOOL

The next three tools, the Paintbrush, the Fountain Pen, and the Pencil, are used exactly as their names imply-for freehand writing or drawing on the screen.

Click on the Paintbrush to select it.

Once you've selected the paintbrush, you can also select any primary color you want to use. You can also change the size and shape of the brush using the Width and Shape workbox.

Move the mouse to the spot where you want to begin painting, then click and drag the mouse to paint with the primary color. Figure 13.9 shows an example of using the Paintbrush.

Figure 13.9 *An example of using the paintbrush.*

THE FOUNTAIN PEN TOOL

Use the Fountain Pen to get smooth, even, freehand shapes using the primary color. If you double-click on the Fountain Pen, you can use the Select a Brush Style dialog box, shown in Figure 13.10, to change the size and shape of the fountain pen.

Figure 13.10 *The Select a Brush Style dialog box.*

You can also change the size and shape of the Fountain Pen using the Width and Shape dialog box.

Once you select the tool, choose the primary color you want to use from the palette. Alternately, you can use the right-hand mouse button to select a color you are already using in your picture, and select it as the primary color.

After you've set all your options, press the left mouse button and drag it over the area to draw freehand with the Fountain Pen.

THE PENCIL TOOL

The Pencil tool works much as it does in CorelDRAW. It is a fly-out menu you can use to draw lines or curves.

1. If you double-click when you select the Pencil tool, the Select a Brush Style dialog box is displayed.

2. Select the style of the point you want to work with.

3. If you click on **Size**, you see the Set Drawing Width dialog box, shown in Figure 13.11. Increase or decrease the width of your line, and also change the units of measure. To help you see what you'll be getting, it also has a preview box that shows you the line width.

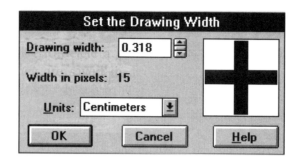

Figure 13.11 *The Set Drawing Width dialog box.*

4. To draw a line, point to where you want to begin the line and drag the mouse to where you want to end the line.

5. Click on the left mouse button to end the line. Figure 13.12 illustrates four lines, of different sizes and colors, placed in the drawing.

Figure 13.12 *Examples of lines.*

THE LINE TOOL

The Line tool creates straight lines by dragging a line on your picture. The **Shift** key may be used to constrain you line to 45-degree increments. There are a couple of special effects you can create using the line tool-joining lines and creating a sunburst effect.

To draw joined lines:

1. Point to where your second line should end and press the right mouse button. A line appears between the end of the first line and where the pointer is positioned.

2. Keeping the right mouse button depressed, position the end of the second line to it's exact position and release the mouse.

Lines can be drawn so that their starting point is joined creating a starburst effect. Using the same method as above, but this time also holding the **Ctrl** key joins the line beginnings.

THE CURVE TOOL

Let's take a look at what the Line tool does when it is in curve mode. When you select the curve, you can choose any primary color you want, and also change the width and shape of the line by using the Width and Shape workbox.

Once the options are selected, you are ready to draw the curve.

1. Select the point where you want the curve to begin. Drag the mouse to the ending point and release the mouse button. A line appears between the two points, with square handles at the ends, and circular handles along the line, as shown in Figure 13.15.

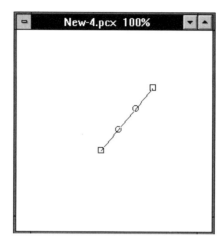

Figure 13.15 *Beginning a curve.*

2. To bend the line into the curved shape that you want, drag one of the circular handles in the direction you want the curve to take.

3. You can further shape the curve by repositioning the end of the curve. To do this, drag on one of the square (end) handles, as shown in Figure 13.16.

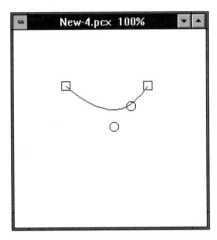

Figure 13.16 *Repositioning the end of a curve.*

4. You can also continue drawing on a curve to create a joined figure. This time you need to use your right mouse button. Point to the area where you want to end the next curve, and click the right mouse button. A new curve segment appears, attached to the end of the first one you drew. You can continue adding on to the end of the curve in this way, until you have created a closed shape, as shown in Figure 13.17.

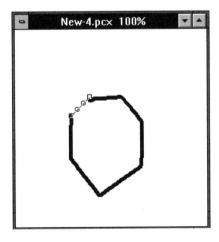

Figure 13.17 *An example of a closed curve.*

NOTE Once your curve is closed, you can use the Paint Roller tool to fill the area, since it is now an enclosed area.

Another trick that you can do with the curve tool is to join curved rays at a single starting point. For this you will also use the right mouse button.

1. Create a simple curve.

2. Point to the area where you want the next curve to end (don't forget that the starting point is the same as the one you used for the first curve).

3. Hold down the **Ctrl** key, and press the right mouse button. A second curve appears.

4. Continue doing this as often as you like, adding a number of curved rays starting at the same point, as shown in Figure 13.18.

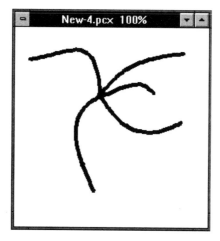

Figure 13.18 *An example of curved rays emanating from a single point.*

5. You can reshape any of the curves you create by dragging on either the circular handles, to change the curvature, or on the square handles, to reposition the end of the curve.

THE ERASER TOOL

If you decide that you don't like any part of what you've drawn, you can use the Eraser to "rub out" a portion of your drawing and change it to the background color. To make it easier to erase, adjust the size and shape of your eraser. Also, before you use the eraser, check to see what background color you've selected (if by chance it's black and you don't realize it, erasing will have a strange effect).

See how the Eraser works by selecting it and erasing the small line in the upper-right corner of your picture.

THE LOCAL UNDO TOOL

Another way of dragging a part of your drawing is by using the Local Undo tool. This tool works like Undo, except instead of undoing the last operation, you can define an area to be undone. This appears in your toolbox as a bottle of "white out," and this is exactly how it works. To show you what effects it has, start with a picture showing paintbrush splotches, as illustrated in Figure 13.13.

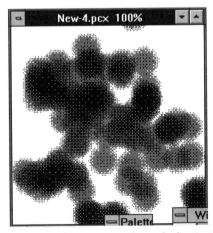

Figure 13.13 *A drawing made with the Paintbrush.*

1. Select the Local Undo tool.

2. Adjust the size and width of the tool in the Width and Shape workbox, to make sure it is large (or small) enough to do what you need.

3. Drag the pointer over the areas of the picture that you want to undo, as shown in Figure 13.14.

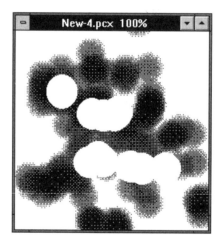

Figure 13.14 *A drawing with Local Undo applied.*

This tool only applies to changes you made since you last selected a tool or command.

N O T E

THE COLOR REPLACER TOOL

This tool looks exactly like the Eraser, except that it has a stroke of color underneath it. When the Color Replacer is selected, it changes the primary color in the area you select to the secondary color.

Before you choose the Color Replacer, make sure you've set both your primary and secondary colors.

N O T E

Before we go on to look at the box tools, let's create a simple work of graffiti on our screen.

1. To make sure that you're starting with a clean slate, select **New** from the File menu, and use the default options for your new picture.

2. Select the Paint Roller tool and choose the Tile Pattern Roller from the fly-out menu.

3. Select **Tile Pattern** from the options menu, and from the file list displayed, select **Bricks**. When you return to your picture, click on your roller in the drawing area. Watch the brick wall appear.

4. Draw a red heart on the brick wall. Select the **Paintbrush** and make sure you've chosen a shade of red as the primary color.

5. From the Width and Shape workbox, set the width to 30, to make sure that it's wide enough to see, then draw the heart.

6. A heart painted on a wall cries out for some initials, so choose the Fountain Pen to write with. Let's select blue as our color.

If you double-click while selecting a color from the palette, you'll see the Adjust Individual Color Palette dialog box, which allows you to modify a particular color.

N O T E

7. Before actually writing the initials on the wall, use the Width and Shape workbox to narrow the width down to 15. Figure 13.19 shows how the photo-painted graffiti is doing.

Figure 13.19 *A red heart and initials drawn on the brick wall.*

8. Finally, select the Eraser and rub out a portion of the picture, to make it look more realistic.

THE HOLLOW BOX TOOLS

Use the Hollow Box tools to create enclosed shapes bordered by the primary color. When you select this tool from the toolbox you have four options, as shown on the fly-out menu in Figure 13.20.

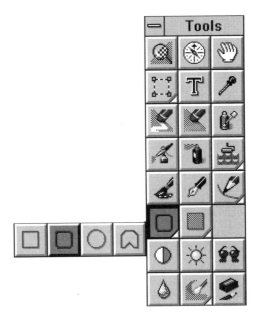

Figure 13.20 *The Hollow Box fly out menu.*

To create a hollow box, rounded box, ellipse, circle, or hollow polygon, follow these steps:

1. Select the shape you want from the fly-out menu.

2. Select the primary color you want for your border.

3. Set the width of the border in the Width and Shape workbox.

4. Move the mouse to where you want the shape to begin, then click and drag until you have the size you want.

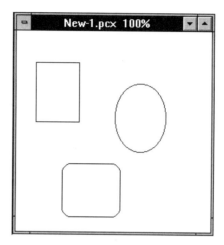

Figure 13.21 *Examples of hollow, ellipse, and rounded hollow boxes.*

When you select the polygon from the Hollow Box fly-out menu, you can create any multisided shape (with up to 200 sides).

1. Make sure you select the primary color you want, and that the width is set properly.

2. Point to where you want to begin the polygon, and click the left mouse button.

3. Point to where you want the first side of the polygon to end and click the left mouse button again.

4. Continue moving the mouse and clicking the left button until the polygon is complete, as shown in Figure 13.22.

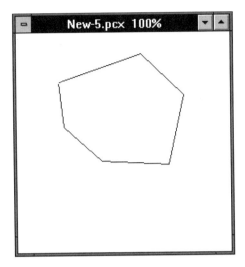

Figure 13.22 *An example of a hollow polygon.*

If you want to constrain the sides of the polygon a 45-degree increment, hold down the **Shift** key.

N O T E

If you wish, you can fill any of these hollow figures using your other painting tools, such as the Spray Can, Airbrush, Paint Roller, Paintbrush, or Fountain Pen.

THE FILLED BOX TOOLS

The Filled Box tools work the same way as the Hollow Box tools, except that they are outlined with the primary color and filled by the secondary color. Select the shape you want from the Filled Box fly-out menu, and check to see that your colors are set the way you want them on the left of the palette.

Use the Width and Shape workbox to set the width of the border. If you do not want a border, set the width to 0.

THE TEXT TOOL

Use the Text tool, shown as a hollow T, to add text to your picture. Because the text is shown in the secondary color, make sure that you have the color you want before you begin. Before you begin entering text, choose a font by clicking on the **Font** menu, then clicking on one of the fonts shown, as illustrated in Figure 13.23.

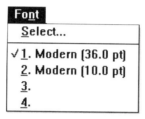

Figure 13.23 *The Font menu.*

If you wish to select a font that isn't shown in the menu, choose **Select**, and the Font dialog box, shown in Figure 13.24 is displayed.

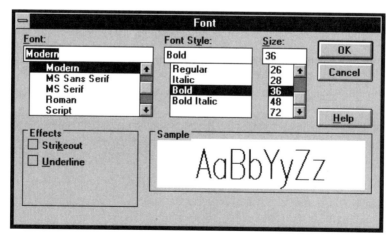

Figure 13.24 *The Font dialog box.*

Select any font installed in Windows. You can also change the type size, and apply any effect, such as bold or underline. When you click on **OK**, the font is selected and added to the Font menu list.

When you have selected your font, click on the **Text tool** from the toolbox, and the Enter Text dialog box is displayed. Use this entry box to type in all the text (up to about 400 characters, or approximately ten lines of text) that you want to add to your picture. Figure 13.25 shows text entered in the Enter Text box.

Figure 13.25 *The Enter Text dialog box.*

Here are some hints for entering text:

1. Text is automatically word-wrapped to the next line.

2. You can paste text from the Windows clipboard by pressing **Shift-Ins**.

3. To break a line in a specific position, press **Ctrl-Enter**.

When you click on **OK**, the text appears in your picture. Click outside the text frame or select a tool to paste the text into the picture as displayed in Figure 13.26.

Figure 13.26 The Text in the Picture.

 Unlike CorelDRAW, you cannot edit the text while it is "in the picture." Before it is pasted into the picture you can get the Enter Text dialog box back by pressing the **Spacebar**.

N O T E

THE EYEDROPPER TOOL

Use the Eyedropper tool to "lift" a color from your picture and replace the primary, secondary, or background color.

1. Click on the Eyedropper tool and point to the color in the picture you want to pick up.

2. Set the color as the primary color by clicking on the left mouse button, the secondary color by clicking on the right mouse button, or the background color by holding the **Shift** key while you click the left mouse button.

THE CLONE TOOL

The Clone tool selects an area and duplicates it within a single picture.

1. Select the Clone tool from the toolbox.

2. Click the right mouse button on the source area.

3. Point to the area where you want to begin cloning and drag using the left mouse button. The cloned image begins appears as you drag.

4. Release the mouse button when the image you wanted appears.

SUMMARY

You have learned how to use the Airbrush, Spray Can, Roller, Paintbrush, Pen, Pencil, Eraser, Local Undo, Color Replacement, Hollow Box, Filled Box, Text, Eyedropper, and Clone tools to modify existing drawings or to add effects of your own.

The next chapter disucsses the CorelPHOTO-PAINT Display and Selection tools, which allow you to view and manipulate your graphics.

CORELPHOTO-PAINT DISPLAY AND SELECTION TOOLS

CorelPHOTO-PAINT has several tools available to let you view and manipulate your work. They let you zoom in and out on an area of your drawing, move your picture, and define areas of your work that you can later cut, copy, or paste. This chapter covers:

▼ The Open command

▼ The Display tools

▼ The Selection tools

251

To illustrate these display and selection tools, we will work with some of the CorelPHOTO-PAINT sample pictures supplied with the software. Let's retrieve one of the pictures now.

THE OPEN COMMAND

Click on the File menu, and select **Open**. The Load a Picture from Disk dialog box, illustrated in Figure 14.1, is displayed.

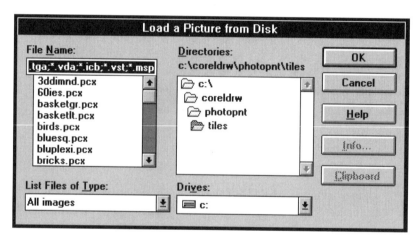

Figure 14.1 *The Load a Picture from Disk dialog box.*

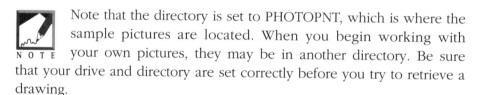 Note that the directory is set to PHOTOPNT, which is where the sample pictures are located. When you begin working with your own pictures, they may be in another directory. Be sure that your drive and directory are set correctly before you try to retrieve a drawing.

Make sure that your File Type is set to *.PCX, and from the list displayed, highlight **Balloon**. Double-click on the name (or click once, then click on **OK**) and the picture is displayed on the CorelPHOTO-PAINT screen, as shown in Figure 14.2.

Figure 14.2 *The balloon picture.*

THE DISPLAY TOOLS

The top row of the toolbox contains the Display tools. These alter the way your picture is displayed on the screen. The Display tools include Zoom, Locator, and Hand.

THE ZOOM TOOL

You may wish to get a close-up of a particular area of your drawing to work with it more accurately. Select the Zoom tool. When the magnification cursor appears, move it over the area you want to zoom in on and press the left mouse button. Try moving it over a portion of the ballon and zooming in, as shown in Figure 14.3.

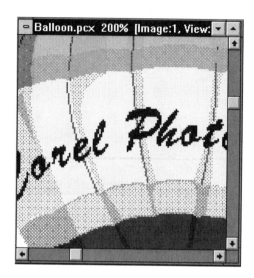

Figure 14.3 *A magnified portion of the balloon picture.*

Every time you click the left mouse button, the magnification increases. To zoom out again, click on the right mouse button. Figure 14.4 shows the balloon picture zoomed out twice.

Figure 14.4 *A zoomed-out balloon picture.*

You can also use the zoom commands in the Display menu to give you more control over the zoom factors.

▼ **Zoom** sets the percentage of magnifications you zoom in.

▼ **100% (No Zoom)** returns you to the 100 percent view.

▼ **Zoom to Fit** displays your picture at desktop size.

THE LOCATOR TOOL

The Locator tool, which looks like a compass, is useful to find a specific location on duplicates of a picture. Click on the Locator tool, then click on the area of the picture you want to see. CorelPHOTO-PAINT displays the area, centered around the area that you clicked, in all copies of the picture.

THE HAND TOOL

Just as when you're drawing manually (remember that?), you may want to move your "paper" around to get a better view of what you're working on. To do so, click on the Hand tool. Then, press the left mouse button and drag the portion of picture into view.

THE SELECTION TOOLS

Use the Selection tools, grouped in the first box of the second row, to define an area of your picture. To see the Selection tools, click on the triangular area in the bottom-right corner of the box, and make your selection from the fly-out, shown in Figure 14.5.

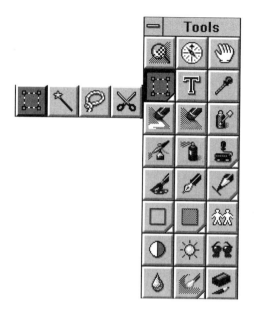

Figure 14.5 *The Selection tools fly-out menu.*

Once you've selected a tool and applied it to a portion of your picture, you can move or resize it, as you did with the Pick tool in CorelDRAW. Using options in the Edit menu, you can also cut, copy, or paste the selected area.

When you define an area of a drawing with one of the selection tools, you can then use the CorelPHOTO-PAINT Gadget Box to manipulate that segment. The Gadget Box is like a marquee with handles on it, as shown in Figure 14.6.

Figure 14.6 *The Gadget Box surrounding a portion of a picture.*

Use the Gadget Box to do the following:

▼ Drag on a corner handle to shrink or stretch.

 Hold down the **Shift** key to resize proportionally.

N O T E

▼ Drag from within the selected portion to move it to another area.

▼ Drag with the left mouse button to make the color opaque.

▼ Drag with the right mouse button to make the color transparent.

▼ Hold the **Shift** key to leave a single copy.

▼ Hold the **Ctrl** key to leave a trail of copies.

Let's go back and look at some of the individual selection tools.

THE BOX SELECTION TOOL

Use the Box Selection tool when you want to define a rectangular area of the picture. Move the mouse to point to a corner of the rectangular area you want to select. Click and drag the mouse until the box encloses the area you want. When you're done, release the mouse button.

If you want to enclose a square area, hold down the **Shift** key while you drag the mouse.

After you've enclosed the area, you can resize it, using the handles on the Gadget Box. Figure 14.7 shows the selected area after it's been stretched.

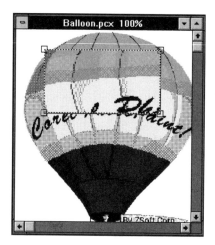

Figure 14.7 *A selected area stretched.*

If you're following on your computer, undo your last action by pressing **Alt-Backspace** (or select **Undo** from the Edit menu) to get a fresh copy of your picture.

THE MAGIC WAND TOOL

The Magic Wand tool defines an area with similar colors that you wish to manipulate. Point to the area you want to define and click the left mouse button. You can then manipulate the area using the Gadget Box.

THE LASSO TOOL

Use the lasso tool to define any irregular portion of a drawing you wish to manipulate.

1. Click on the Lasso from the selection tools.

2. Click the left mouse button and drag the mouse over the area you want to "rope in." When the area is enclosed, release the mouse button.

3. Once you've lassoed the area, you can drag it to another portion of your drawing.

THE SCISSORS TOOL

Use the Scissors tool to define a portion of your drawing in a polygon shape that you wish to work with.

1. Click on the Scissors from the selection tools.

2. Point to one corner of the area that you wish to select and press the left mouse button.

3. Move the mouse to the end of the first side of the polygon and click again.

4. Continue until you have defined all of the sides of the polygon. Figure 14.8 shows a triangular area defined with the Scissors.

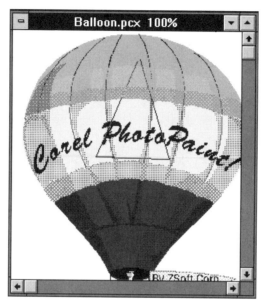

Figure 14.8 Using the Scissors tool.

 You can also define the area by dragging the mouse. If you want to constrain (restrict) the size of the angle to 45 degrees, hold down the **Shift** key while you drag over the area.

Now that you have the area defined, you can use some of the options from the Edit menu. To cut the area out of your drawing, select **Cut** from the Edit menu. The triangular area is removed from your drawing, as shown in Figure 14.9.

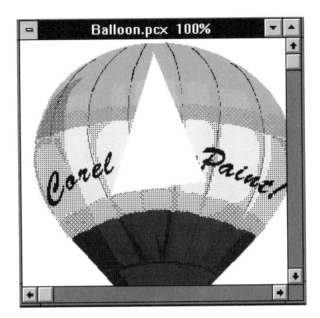

Figure 14.9 *Cutting an area from the drawing.*

When you cut a portion from your drawing, it is placed into the Windows Clipboard. The contents of the Clipboard can be used in other Corel applications, as well as any other Windows applications.

Since placing a portion of a picture in the Clipboard occupies additional memory, select **Delete** from the Edit menu if you wish only to erase the segment from your picture but do not wish to use it later.

The Copy option from the Edit menu works almost exactly like the Cut option because the defined area is placed on the Windows Clipboard. However, the copied portion remains in your drawing.

You can paste whatever is in the Windows Clipboard back to your drawing at any time. Select **Paste** from the Edit menu, and the area that you save is pasted into the upper-left corner of your picture, as shown in Figure 14.10.

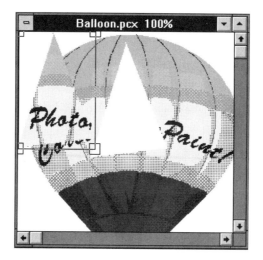

Figure 14.10 *Pasting the contents of the Clipboard into your drawing.*

SUMMARY

You've now learned how to:

▼ Open a CorelPHOTO-PAINT file.

▼ Use the display tools to zoom in or out on a portion of your drawing, locate the same area in duplicates of a drawing, and move the view of your drawing within the display window.

▼ Use the Selection tools, the Selection box, the Magic Wand, the Lasso, and the Scissors, to define an area of your drawing.

▼ Use the Gadget Box to move, stretch, shrink, skew, and copy the selected portion of your drawing.

▼ Use the cut, copy, and paste options from the Edit menu to move selected portions in and out of your drawing, to and from the Windows clipboard.

CORELPHOTO-PAINT RETOUCHING TOOLS

The last group of in tools CorelPHOTO-PAINT are the Retouching tools, found on the bottom row of the CorelPHOTO-PAINT toolbox. You may find these tools particularly helpful if you're working with photographs or other work you've scanned into your system. These retouch images by blending, tinting, smudging, or smearing an area. These tools also brighten or change the contrast in areas of your picture. This chapter covers:

▼ The Contrast Paintbrush tool.

▼ The Brighten Paintbrush tool.

▼ The Tint Paintbrush tool.

▼ The Blend Paintbrush tool.

▼ The Smear Paintbrush tool.

▼ The Smudge Paintbrush tool.

▼ The Sharpen Paintbrush tool.

263

All of the Retouching tools have a cursor that lets you retouch any area of the picture currently on the screen. As you did with the drawing tools, you can use the Width & Shape workbox to adjust the size and shape of the retouching tools. Use a lower number if you are retouching a smaller area, or a higher number if you want to work on a larger portion of the picture.

To illustrate these display and selection tools, we will work with one of the CorelPHOTO-PAINT sample pictures supplied with the software. Click on the **File** menu, and select **Open**. From the Open dialog box, select PAINTWAY.PCX, and the picture is displayed on your CorelPHOTO-PAINT screen, as illustrated in Figure 15.1.

Figure 15.1 *PAINTWAY.PCX opened.*

Be sure the directory is set to PHOTOPNT, which is where the sample pictures are located.

THE CONTRAST PAINTBRUSH TOOL

The Contrast Paintbrush tool increases the contrast of any area in your drawing by brightening or darkening any areas.

To use the Contrast Paintbrush, click on it. The Palette workbox is displayed, which allows you to increase or decrease the amount of contrast created by the Contrast Paintbrush.

You can change the values in the Palette workbox by clicking on the scroll bar, dragging the arrow in the workbox, or typing in a number.

Drag the Paintbrush over the area that you want to change. Figures 15.2 and 15.3 show the Contrast Paintbrush using a -95 and +95 percent contrasts.

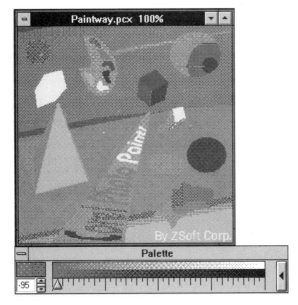

Figure 15.2 *PAINTWAY.PCX with -95 percent contrast.*

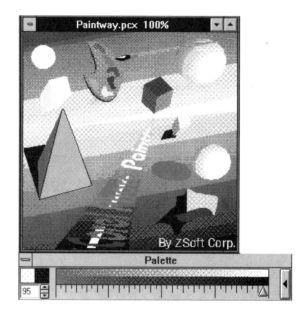

Figure 15.3 *PAINTWAY.PCX with +95 percent contrast.*

Only the first pass over the area with the paintbrush changes the area. You can select the Contrast Paintbrush again (and adjust the Palette if you need to) to achieve additional contrast.

THE BRIGHTEN PAINTBRUSH TOOL

The Brighten Paintbrush tool lets you change the intensity of all colors (except black or white). This tool lets you lighten an area to add highlights, or darken an area to add shadows. Figure 15.4 shows Brighten Paintbrush applied to PAINTWAY.PCX.

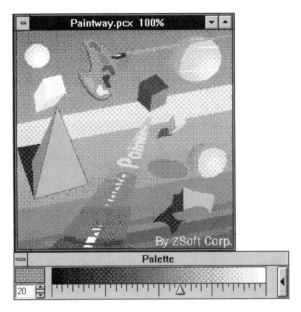

Figure 15.4 PAINTWAY.PCX *with Brighten Paintbrush applied.*

Use the Palette workbox the same way as with the Contrast Paintbrush. Positive numbers brighten the area in your picture and negative numbers darken it.

THE TINT PAINTBRUSH TOOL

The Tint Paintbrush tool alters the colors in an area by applying a type of tinted "filter" it.

Before you use the Tint Paintbrush tool on a gray scale picture, convert your picture to 24-bit color. Select **Convert To** from the Edit menu, and then select **24-Bit Color**. Figure 15.5 shows the Convert To option.

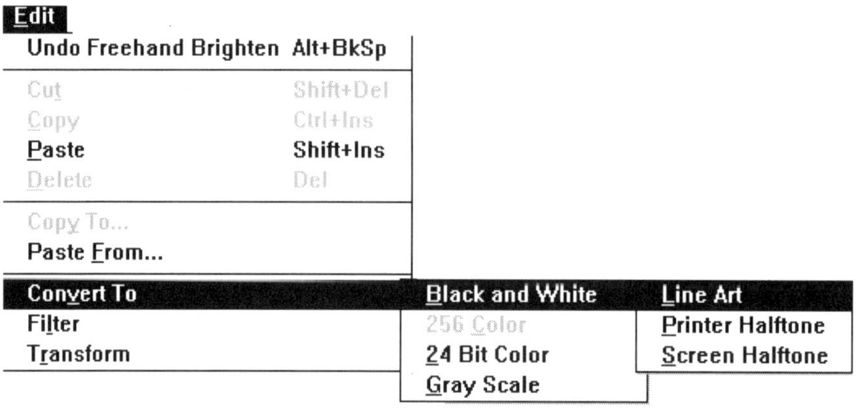

```
┌─────────────┐
│ Edit        │
├─────────────────────────────────────────────┐
│ Undo Freehand Brighten   Alt+BkSp            │
│                                              │
│ Cut                      Shift+Del           │
│ Copy                     Ctrl+Ins            │
│ Paste                    Shift+Ins           │
│ Delete                   Del                 │
│                                              │
│ Copy To...                                   │
│ Paste From...                                │
├──────────────────────┬───────────────────┬──────────────────┐
│ Convert To           │ Black and White   │ Line Art         │
│ Filter               │ 256 Color         │ Printer Halftone │
│ Transform            │ 24 Bit Color      │ Screen Halftone  │
│                      │ Gray Scale        │                  │
```

Figure 15.5 *The Convert To option from the Edit menu.*

When you select the Tint Paintbrush tool, be sure you have selected the primary color that you want to use as your filter. Once you're certain that the brush is the correct size and shape, drag the mouse over the part of the picture you want to change. Figure 15.6 shows the result of using the Tint Paintbrush option.

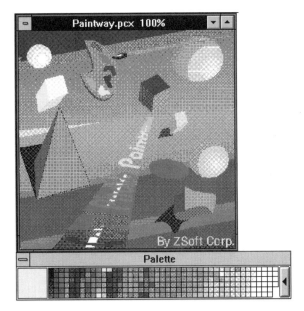

Figure 15.6 *PAINTWAY.PCX with the Tint Paintbrush applied.*

THE BLEND PAINTBRUSH TOOL

Use the Blend Paintbrush tool to smooth and soften transitions by blending two adjacent areas in 24-bit color or gray-scale picture. Like the Contrast Paintbrush and Brighten Paintbrush tools, you can use the Palette workbox to achieve a smoother effect (higher number) or sharper effect (lower number). Unlike the previous Retouching tools we've discussed, you can go over an area multiple times until you get the blend that you want. Figure 15.7 shows the effect of using the Blend Paintbrush.

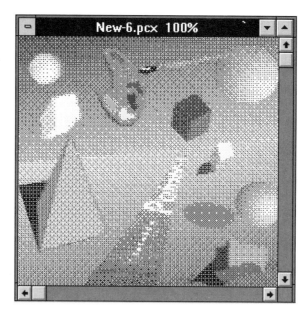

Figure 15.7 *PAINTWAY.PCX with the Blend Paintbrush applied.*

THE SMEAR PAINTBRUSH TOOL

Use the Smear Paintbrush tool to spread colors in your picture. Remember that you can adjust the brush with the Width and Shape workbox. You can also choose **Soft Brush Settings** from the Options menu (which we described when we discussed the drawing tools) to change the effect of the brush.

To get the Soft Brush Settings dialog box, you can also double-click on the Smear Paintbrush tool.

When you select the **Smear Paintbrush**, you can go over the selected area of your picture several times, until you have the result that you want. Figure 15.8 shows the effects of the Smear Paintbrush (see the upper-right portion of the drawing).

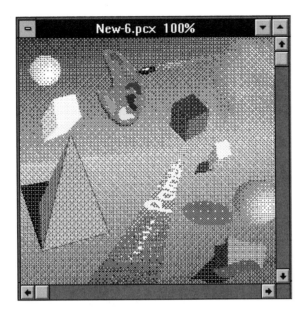

Figure 15.8 PAINTWAY.PCX with the Smear Paintbrush applied.

The Smear Paintbrush is a grouped tool, together with the Smudge Spray Can. Click on the triangle in the lower-right corner to make your selection from the fly-out menu.

THE SMUDGE SPRAY CAN TOOL

The Smudge Spray Can is another tool for softening the edges in your picture. Just as with its "sister" tool, the Smear Paintbrush, you can drag over an area several times until you get the degree of smudging you need. Figure 15.9 shows the effects of the Smudge Spray can, which has blurred the horizon line.

Figure 15.9 *PAINTWAY.PCX with the Smudge Spray Can applied to the horizon.*

Remember that the Smudge Spray Can is grouped with the Smear Paintbrush. If you don't see it in your toolbox, click on the triangle in the lower right corner and make your selection from the fly-out menu.

THE SHARPEN PAINTBRUSH TOOL

Use the Sharpen Paintbrush tool to sharpen areas of your picture that may be too "fuzzy." Use the Palette workbox to create a sharper effect (higher number) or a smoother effect (lower number).

The Sharpen Paintbrush lets you go over an area multiple times, until you have the effect you want. Figure 15.10 shows the Sharpen Paintbrush applied to the bottom edge of the pyramid.

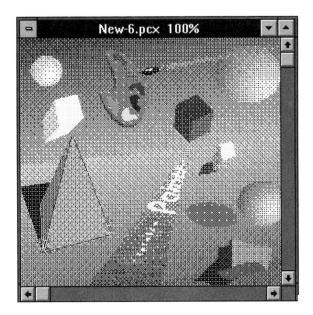

Figure 15.10 *PAINTWAY.PCX with the Sharpen Paintbrush applied to the pyramid.*

SUMMARY

You've now learned how to use the CorelPHOTO-PAINT Retouching tools to correct and fine-tune your pictures by sharpening or smoothing areas of your drawing or photo, increasing or decreasing contrast, or applying tint. These tools also let you blend or brighten your picture, and even control the degree of retouching you need.

CORELCHART

This chapter discusses:

- ▼ Some fundamentals
- ▼ The toolbar
- ▼ The menus

There are two main elements in CorelCHART.

▼ The Data Manager enters and formats numeric and text data.

▼ Chart View transforms the data into a chart or a graph.

CorelCHART imports spreadsheet data created in other applications, such as Lotus 1-2-3 and Microsoft Excel.

You must have Windows 3.1 installed to use True Type fonts and to take advantage of the Object Linking and Embedding (OLE) features of the application.

SOME FUNDAMENTALS

The CorelCHART screen is basically laid out in the same format as the other Corel applications. Figure 16.1 shows the basic CorelCHART screen.

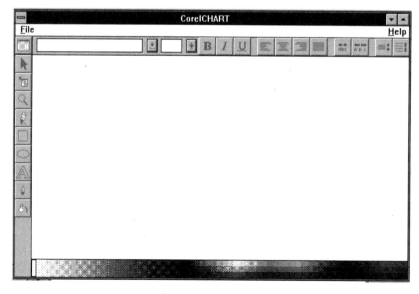

Figure 16.1 *The CorelCHART screen.*

It consists of a Title bar, a Menu bar, which contains several drop-down menus, a Toolbar, which appears very similar to the CorelDRAW Toolbox, and the Text Ribbon, which allows you to control the font size and style of the text you'll be using in your chart. The bottom of your screen displays a color palette, convenient for interactively assigning colors to your chart elements.

THE CHART

There are several elements that make up every chart that you work with. Let's look at Figure 16.2 which identifies the different parts of a CorelCHART chart.

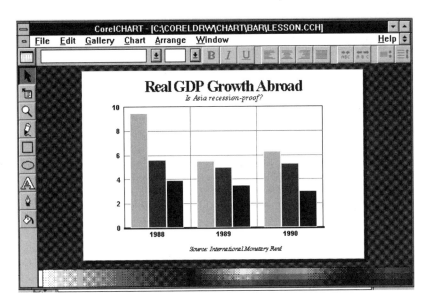

Figure 16.2 *A CorelCHART chart.*

This is useful as we discuss charting and manipulating the data in a chart.

Although it looks one-dimensional, a chart consists of two layers. The chart layer contains the titles, footnotes, legends, axis scales, and access titles. The annotation layer is for graphics and other information you add to highlight the features on the chart, in other words, to further explain your chart.

THE TOOLBAR

The top button of the toolbar toggles between the Data Manager, where you'll be entering or importing data to use in your charts, and the Chart View, where you can see your chart. Only through the Data Manager can you access the numbers and other data that make up your chart. If you've used an electronic spreadsheet before, you will be very comfortable working in the CorelCHART Data Manager.

THE PICK TOOL

Use the Pick tool to select, size, scale, or move an object. If you hold the **Ctrl** key while stretching or scaling, you can stretch or scale in 100-percent increments, and if you hold the **Shift** key while stretching an object, you can stretch an object in two directions, outward from its center. However, because you're working with charts, holding the **Ctrl** key while you move an object keeps the object along either the horizontal or vertical axis.

THE CONTEXT SENSITIVE POP-UP MENU TOOL

The next tool is the Context Sensitive pop-up menu tool. This tool accesses the menu that controls whichever chart element you are working on. Although you can get to all these options via the main menu bar, this tool allows you to see all the items relevant to the particular item that you selected in the same place. Figure 16.3 shows the Context Sensitive pop-up menus for the Title the Bar Riser.

Figure 16.3 *The Context Sensitive pop-up menu for the title.*

After selecting the chart element you wish to change, click the right mouse button to access the Context Sensitive pop-up menu.

SHORT CUT

THE ZOOM TOOL

The Zoom tool gives you a fly-out menu, shown in Figure 16.4, that controls the size of the viewing window. The Zoom tool allows you to keep your screen at window size, reduce the viewing area to 25 percent or 50 percent of window size, or magnify the screen to 100 percent, 200 percent, or 400 percent of window size.

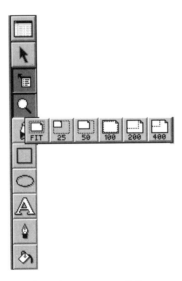

Figure 16.4 *The Zoom tool fly-out menu.*

THE PENCIL TOOL

The Pencil tool also presents a fly-out menu, shown in Figure 16.5. The first item in the fly-out allows you to draw straight lines, in the same manner as you used in CorelDRAW.

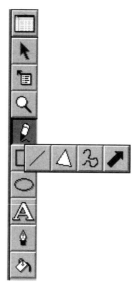

Figure 16.5 *The Pencil tool fly-out menu.*

The second option draws polygons. Click on the location where you want your shape to begin, then move (but do not drag) the mouse to the next location and click. Proceed until your polygon is complete.

The third option controls freehand drawing, as with the freehand pencil tool in CorelDRAW.

The arrow draws arrows. Click on the point where you want the arrow to begin, and then drag the mouse to the point where you want the arrow to end. If you wish to change the style of the arrow, use the Context Sensitive pop-up menu.

THE RECTANGLE AND ELLIPSE TOOLS

The Rectangle and Ellipse tools work exactly like their equivalents in CorelDRAW. Simply click at the location where you want the object to begin, drag the mouse to the ending point, and release it.

Holding the **Ctrl** key while you drag with your mouse transforms rectangles and ellipses to squares and circles, respectively.

N O T E

THE TEXT TOOL

Use the Text tool to enter text for chart annotations. To add text:

1. Click on the Text tool.

2. Move the mouse to the location where you want to begin your text, and click and drag until you've created a paragraph frame large enough to hold all your text, as shown in Figure 16.6.

3. Once you've entered your text, use the Text Ribbon to change the typeface, style, and size of the text.

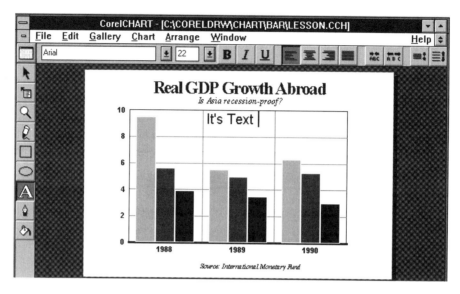

Figure 16.6 *A paragraph frame for text.*

You can also use the Text tool to edit text in the Titles, Subtitles, and Footnotes.

THE OUTLINE TOOL

The Outline tool works like its CorelDRAW counterpart. You can choose a line width, color, or shades of gray for your outline, or you can elect to use no outline. The Outline fly-out menu is shown in Figure 16.7.

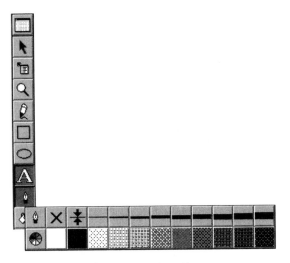

Figure 16.7 *The Outline fly-out menu.*

THE FILL TOOL

The Fill tool fly-out menu, shown in Figure 16.8, offers several options.

Figure 16.8 *The Fill fly-out menu.*

The Color Wheel lets you choose a color for the selected element.

The Quick Pick displays a menu, shown in Figure 16.9, that lets you store and access hatch patterns, fountain fills, and bitmap patterns you can use to fill an element. To use the tool, scroll on the arrow at the top of the box to see the list of fills available. You can also use the forward and back buttons at the bottom to scroll through the previews. Once you've made your selection, click on **Apply** to actually apply the element.

Figure 16.9 *The Quick Pick menu.*

Select **Nofill X** in the quick pick menus for vector graphics, bitmaps, and found box to eliminate the fill from an object. The next three boxes attain fills, respectively.

The options on the bottom row of the fly-out menu let you choose black, white, or preset pattern fills for the selected elements. The preset patterns are convenient for distinguishing the different bars of a bar chart, for example.

THE MENUS

THE FILE MENU

The File menu, shown in Figure 16.10, manages CorelCHART files on disk. Begin a new file by accessing one of the standard chart templates, open an existing file, or write a chart out to disk. Options in the File menu also control the printing of charts.

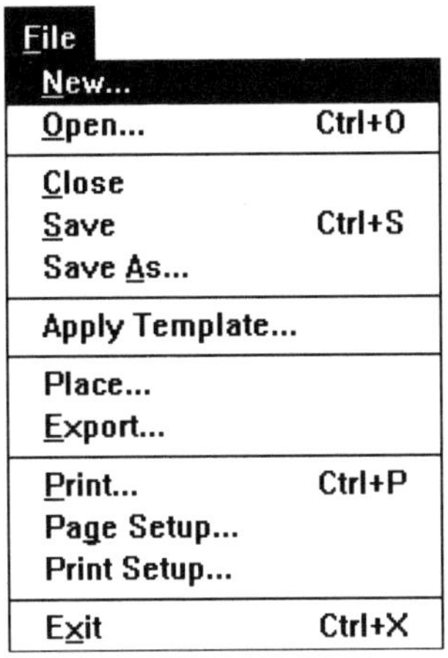

File	
New...	
Open...	Ctrl+O
Close	
Save	Ctrl+S
Save As...	
Apply Template...	
Place...	
Export...	
Print...	Ctrl+P
Page Setup...	
Print Setup...	
Exit	Ctrl+X

Figure 16.10 *The File menu.*

You can import charts from other applications in the following formats:

▼ ASCII (values separated by commas   *.CSV

▼ ASCII (values separated by spaces or tabs *.TXT

▼ dBase   *.DBF

▼ Excel spreadsheet   *.XLS

| ▼ Harvard | *.CHT |
| ▼ Lotus | *.WK1, *.WK3 |

You can also import graphics images in these formats:

▼ CorelTRACE	*.EPS
▼ CorelPHOTO-PAINT	*.PCX ,*PCC
▼ Windows Paintbrush	*.PCX ,*.PCC
▼ Windows Bitmap	*.BMP
▼ Windows Metafile	*.WMF
▼ AutoCAD DXF	*.DXF
▼ CompuServe Bitmap	*.GIF
▼ Computer Graphics	*CGM
▼ GEM	*.GEM
▼ HP Plotter HPGL	*.PLT
▼ IBM PIF	*.PIF
▼ Lotus PIC	* PIC
▼ Mac PICT	*.PCT
▼ Illustrator 88, 3.0	*.AI, *.EPS
▼ TARGA bitmap	*.TGA
▼ Tiff 5.0 bitmap	*.TIF

If you wish to use your charts in other applications, you can export them using these graphics file formats:

▼ CorelPHOTO-PAINT	*.PCX
▼ Windows Paintbrush	*.PCX
▼ Windows Bitmap	*.BMP
▼ AutoCAD DXF	*.DXF

▼	CompuServe Bitmap	*.GIF
▼	Computer Graphics	*.CGM
▼	GEM files	*.GEM
▼	Encapsulated Postscript	*.EPS
▼	HP Plotter HPGL	*PLT
▼	IBM PIF	*.PIF
▼	Illustrator 88 3.0	*.AI, *EPS
▼	Mac PICT	*.PCT
▼	TARGA Bitmap	*.TGA
▼	Tiff 5.0 Bitmap	*.TIF
▼	WordPerfect Graphic	*.WPG
▼	Lotus PIC	*.PIC

THE EDIT MENU

Use the Edit menu, shown in Figure 16.11, to Undo your last action, duplicate your CorelCHART elements, or Cut, Copy, or Paste to and from the Windows Clipboard.

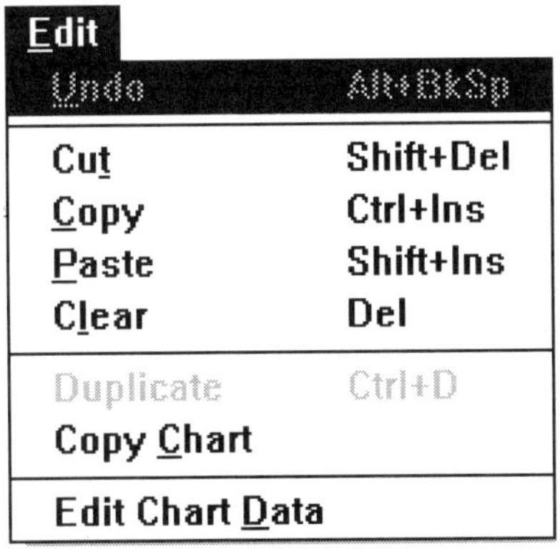

Figure 16.11 *The Edit menu.*

THE GALLERY MENU

The Gallery menu, shown in Figure 16.12 lets you select a chart type, and choose a variation on the chart type.

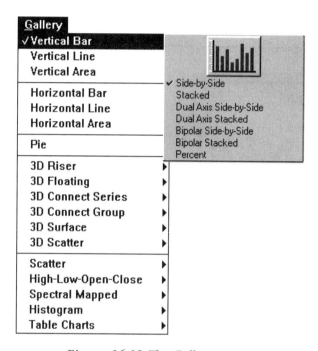

Figure 16.12 *The Gallery menu.*

THE CHART MENU

The options on the Chart menu manipulate the placement and appearance of items on your chart. The menu selections vary with the type of chart in the active window.

THE ARRANGE MENU

The Arrange menu, shown in Figure 16.13, works like its CorelDRAW counterpart, letting you bring elements in front of or behind other elements.

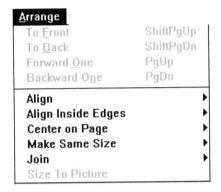

Figure 16.13 *The Arrange menu.*

THE WINDOW MENU

The Window menu arranges your screen display, to make a more workable arrangement.

SUMMARY

In this chapter, you've had a quick tour of some of the CorelCHART basics. You learned:

▼ How CorelCHART works.

▼ The CorelCHART toolbox, including the Data Manager and the Chart Views, the Pick tool, the Context Sensitive pop-up tool, and Pencil tool, and the Rectangle and Ellipse tools, the Text tool, the Outline tool, and the Fill tools.

▼ The CorelCHART menu bar, including the File, Edit, Gallery, Chart, and Arrange menus.

CHAPTER

17

THE CORELCHART DATA MANAGER

To create charts using CorelCHART, you need to begin with the data that will make up your chart. To do this, you'll need to work with the Data Manager, the matrix into which you import or enter the basic information that generates in your chart. This chapter covers:

▼ The Data Manager matrix.

▼ Importing data.

▼ Entering information in the matrix.

▼ Tagging cells.

▼ Moving and reformatting information.

291

THE DATA MANAGER MATRIX

If you've ever worked with an electronic spreadsheet, the Data Manager screen display, shown in Figure 17.1, will look very familiar to you. It consists of columns, each headed by a letter of the alphabet, and rows, each beginning with a number. A cell exists at each intersection of a column and a row, and is shown as a small box on the screen. Each cell has a location, which can be addressed by its row letter and column number. For example, the cell in the upper-left corner of the matrix is cell A1.

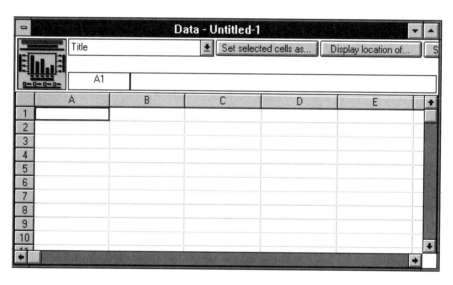

Figure 17.1 *The Data Manager screen.*

ANATOMY OF THE MATRIX

Most of the screen consists of the cells that make up your matrix. However, there are other elements that help you work in the Data Manager. Directly under the Menu Bar is the text ribbon, which you can use to specify the typeface, size, style, and justification of the text that you enter into the matrix. Directly underneath that, you'll see a bar that displays the Tag List. By clicking on the down arrow, you'll see a list of all of the types of Data Manager tags, as shown in Figure 17.2.

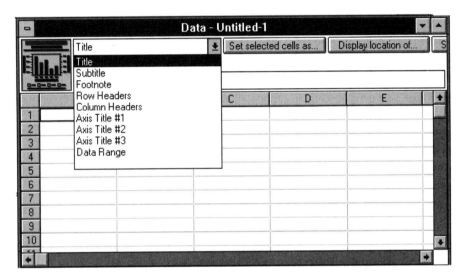

Figure 17.2 The Tag list.

The **Set selected cells as** button, just to the right, works the same way as the **OK** or **Apply** buttons you've used until now. It applies an option (such as a tag name you've selected from a Tag List) to a group of selected elements. The **Display location of** button helps you find data of a specific type. For example, if you click on **Subtitle** from the Tag List, then click on **Display location of**, the Data Manager highlights the cell that contains the subtitle.

ACCESSING THE DATA MANAGER

You can access the data manager either by clicking on the **Data Manager** button at the top of the toolbar, or by selecting **Edit Chart Data** from the Edit menu.

N O T E   Once you're working in Data Manager, the Data Manager tool transforms into the Chart View tool. In other words, this tool is a toggle, that lets you switch back and forth between the Data Manager and the Chart View.

WORKING WITH CELLS

To select one particular cell, point to the cell with your mouse and click on it. If you wish to select a range of adjoining cells, click on one of the corner cells, and drag your mouse to the diagonally opposite corner, as shown in Figure 17.3.

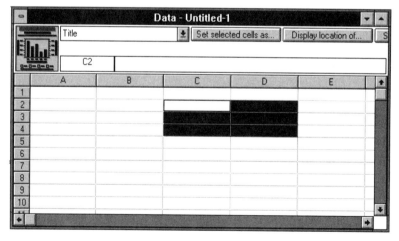

Figure 17.3 *Selecting adjacent cells.*

If you wish to select a group of noncontiguous cells, click on each cell you want to select while holding down the **Ctrl** key. Figure 17.4 shows a group of nonadjacent cells selected.

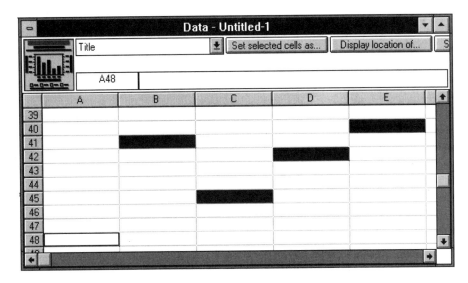

Figure 17.4 *Selecting nonadjacent cells.*

BEGINNING A NEW CHART

Before we can work with the Data Manager, we'll need to begin building a new chart.

Unlike an electronic spreadsheet, where the information is the basis of the application and the graphic representation follows, CorelCHART is based on the chart—the data in the Data Manager serves to support the representation of that information.

N O T E

To build a new chart, select **New** from the File menu. The New dialog box, shown in Figure 17.5, is displayed.

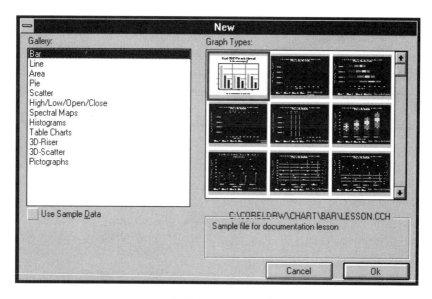

Figure 17.5 *The New dialog box.*

If you wish to enter your own data and not use the sample data as a template, click off the **Use Sample Data** checkbox. Then select a chart type from the gallery listed in the left side of the dialog box. The gallery previews, graphically displayed on the right side of the dialog box, will help you make your selection.

Click on **OK**, and the Data Manager matrix is displayed on the screen. However, as you can see in Figure 17.6, the matrix is blank. You have to either import chart data or begin entering data before you can actually show a chart.

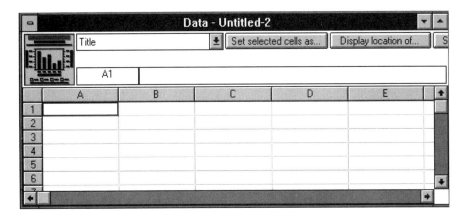

Figure 17.6 *A blank Data Manager matrix.*

IMPORTING DATA

Very often you'll want to chart data that you've already entered into an electronic spreadsheet, and perhaps made mathematical analysis on. Therefore, you'll need the capacity to import a spreadsheet into CorelCHART.

To import a data file into CorelCHART, select **Import** from the File menu. The Import File with File Type dialog box, shown in Figure 17.7, is displayed.

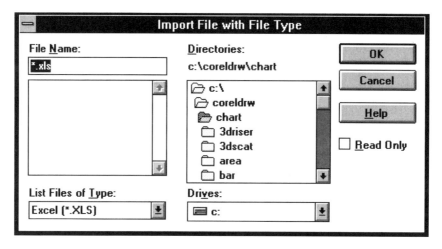

Figure 17.7 *Import File with File Type dialog box.*

From the List Files of Type box, select the type of file that you wish to import. Locate the correct drive and directory where your data is stored, and from the list of files shown under the File Name box, click on the filename of the box that you want, and click on **OK**. Your data is displayed in the Data Manager matrix, as shown in Figure 17.8.

	A	B	C	D	E	F
1	Real GDP Growth					
2	Is Asia recession-p					
3	Source: Internatior					
4		1988	1989	1990	1991	
5	NICS	9.5	5.5	6.3		
6	Japan	5.6	5	5.3		
7	EC	3.9	3.5	3		
8						
9						

Data - Untitled-2 — Title — Set selected cells as... — Display location of... — Scan Data — A1 — Real GDP Growth Abroad

Figure 17.8 *A Data Manager matrix with imported data.*

ENTERING INFORMATION IN THE MATRIX

If you have not imported data, you may need to enter all of your data from scratch. However, you may also want to enter additional information to add to the data you've already imported. Now that you know what rows, columns, and cells are, we can discuss entering information in the data manager.

To select the cell where you want to enter or change data, simply click on the cell with your mouse. Alternately, you can move your cursor into the cell using the **Arrow** key. Once you've entered the data for that cell, you can move on to the next cell you need, either by using the arrow keys or by selecting it with the mouse.

The Contents Box just above the Column Letters, displays the cell address on the left side, and the data as you type it on the right side.

N O T E

TAGGING CELLS

Before you can use any of this information in a chart, you'll need to tag the cells you want charted. This lets CorelCHART know what each cell (or group of cells) will be used for. CorelCHART has established a few defaults, groups of cells that are already tagged for you. These are:

▼ **A1** Title.

▼ **A2** Subtitle.

▼ **A3** Footnote.

▼ **A5...** Row headers (begin them in A5, and proceed downward).

▼ **B4...** Column headers (begin them in B4, and proceed to the right).

▼ **B5...** Data range (begin entering data in B5, and proceed across and down).

You may need to assign tags to other groups of cells in your matrix, for example, to tag the data axis titles. To tag a cell or group of cells, follow these steps:

1. Select the cell or group of cells you wish to tag.

2. From the Tag List, click on the type of tag you need. The Tag is highlighted.

3. Click on the **Set selected cells as** button, and the selected cells are tagged.

NOTE   If you've imported data, some of the elements may be already tagged. To see what, if any, tags are applied, click on a tag from the Tag List, then click on **Display location of**. The cells that are assigned to the selected tag are displayed, as shown in Figure 17.9.

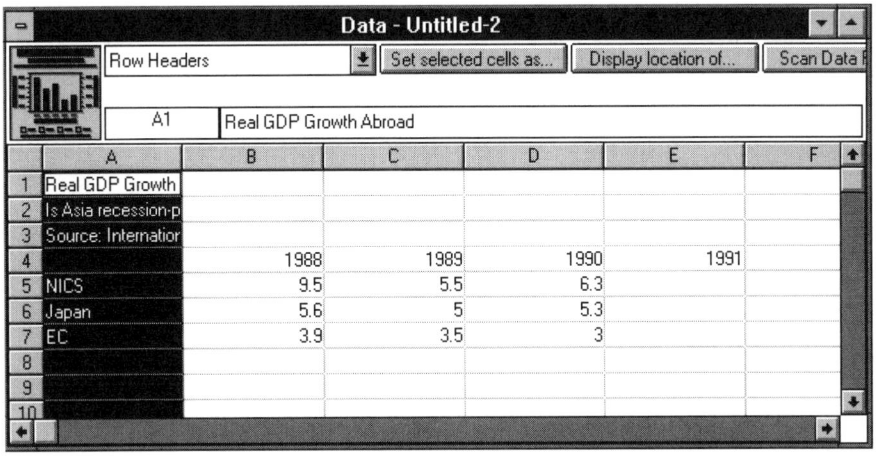

Figure 17.9 *Displaying the location of row headers.*

MOVING AND REFORMATTING INFORMATION

After you've imported or entered information into the Data Manager matrix, you may find that you want to relocate some of the information. You may also find that you need to resize the cells to accommodate your data, sort the information, or exchange cell data for column data. Here's how it's done.

MOVING AND COPYING CELLS

In the Data Manager, you can move or copy any cell or group of cells by using the Copy, Cut, and Paste options from the Edit menu. Select the cell or group of cells that you wish to copy or move.

If you wish to *copy* the group of cells (in other words, have the information appear in two locations in the matrix), select **Copy** from the Edit menu. Then, move the mouse or **Arrow** keys to the cell (or the beginning cell) where you'd like to place the information, and select **Paste** from the Edit menu. The selected cells are copied at the new location.

If, you'd like to *move* data (that is, have it appear at the new location only), choose **Cut** from the Edit menu after you've selected your cells. Then point to the new location and choose **Paste**. The data is moved to the new location.

When you begin a new chart in the Data Manager, all columns are the same width. However, you may need to change the width of a column, for example, to accommodate longer text elements, such as titles, subtitles, and footnotes. To resize a column, move the cursor into the gap between the column headers until it changes from a crosshair to a vertical bar with arrows. Click and drag right or left to move the dividing line between the columns. This changes the width of the columns, as shown in Figure 17.10.

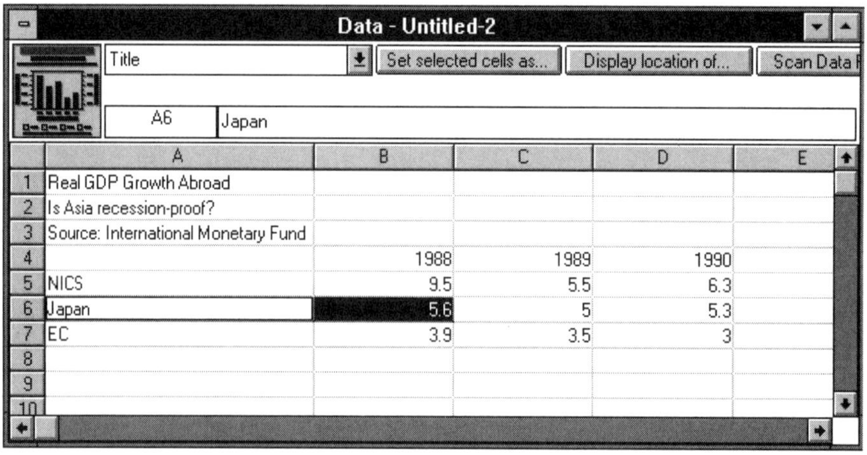
Data - Untitled-2
Title
Set selected cells as...
Display location of...
Scan Data
A6
Japan
A
B
C
D
E
1 Real GDP Growth Abroad
2 Is Asia recession-proof?
3 Source: International Monetary Fund
4 1988 1989 1990
5 NICS 9.5 5.5 6.3
6 Japan 5.6 5 5.3
7 EC 3.9 3.5 3
8
9
10

Figure 17.10 *Column A resized.*

SORTING DATA

You may wish to sort data to rearrange the information in a group of related cells. For example, if you have a group of names, you may wish to sort them in alphabetical order.

To begin, select the group of cells that you wish to sort, then select **Sort** from the Data menu. The Sort dialog box, shown in Figure 17.11, is displayed.

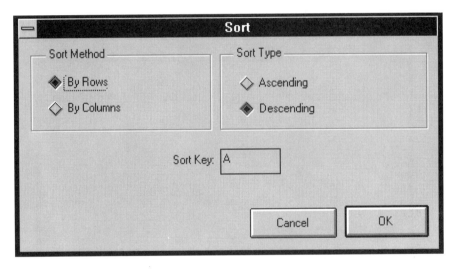

Figure 17.11 *The Sort dialog box.*

If you wish to sort the Rows within a Column, click on **By Rows** and enter the Column letter in the Sort Key. If, however, you wish to sort the Columns within a Row, click on **By Columns**, and enter the Row number in the Sort Key.

To sort the data in Ascending sequence, from lowest to highest, click on **Ascending**. To sort in backwards order, click on **Descending**. When you've completed all of the information in the dialog box, click on **OK**, and the specified data is sorted.

SWAPPING DATA LOCATIONS

To make it easier to set up data ranges, you may wish to swap or exchange rows or columns of data. For example, in the matrix shown, let's swap the data in rows 5 and 7. Choose **Exchange** from the Data menu. The Exchange dialog box, shown in Figure 17.12, is displayed.

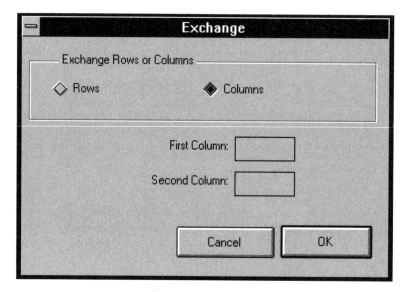

Figure 17.12 *The Exchange dialog box.*

Click on either **Rows** or **Columns** to specify whether you'll be exchanging rows or columns. Then enter the row or column numbers of the columns you wish to swap. In this case, we'll enter 5 and 7.

The rows and columns do not need to be adjacent to be swapped.

N O T E

When you've completed all of the information in the dialog box, click on **OK**, and the specified rows or columns are exchanged. Figure 17.13 shows rows 5 and 7 swapped.

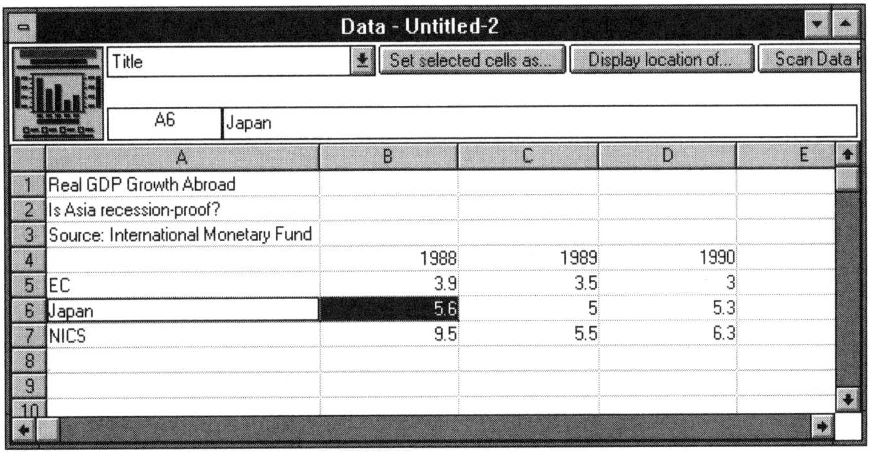

Figure 17.13 *Rows 5 and 7 swapped.*

SUMMARY

In this chapter we've explored some of the basics of the Data Manager, the foundation underlying the charts that you can build with CorelCHART. You have learned:

▼ The layout of the Data Manager matrix.

▼ Selecting cells.

▼ Importing information into the Data Manager.

▼ Entering data into the Data Manager matrix.

▼ Working with cell tags.

▼ Moving, Formatting, Resizing, Sorting, and Swapping Data Manager information.

CHARTING WITH CORELCHART

Now that you've learned some of the fundamentals of CorelCHART, let's look at what this application is all about—making charts. CorelCHART can display a variety of charts, giving you the ability to represent different types of data to their best advantage.

This chapter covers:

▼ Beginning a chart.

▼ Changing a chart's appearance.

▼ Selecting the best chart type.

307

BEGINNING A CHART

Before we learn how to display data on a chart, let's review some of the fundamentals of beginning a chart. To start a new chart:

1. Select **New** from the File menu. The New dialog box, shown in Figure 18.1, is displayed.

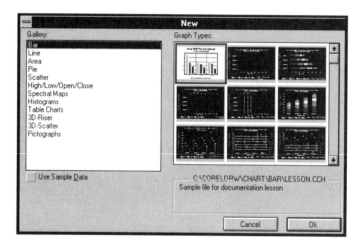

Figure 18.1 *The New dialog box.*

2. From the Gallery list, select the chart type that you want. In the first example, we'll be using a bar chart. Once you select a chart type, you'll see a Data Manager screen, but it will be blank because you haven't yet entered or imported any data.

3. To add some data, select **Import** from the File menu.

4. The chart we'll be working with uses one of the sample files, LESSON.XLS. Since this is an Excel spreadsheet, make sure that the List Files of Type box is set to Excel (*.XLS), and select the file from the file box. Click on **OK** and the data is displayed in the Data Manager, as shown in Figure 18.2.

	A	B	C	D	E	
1	Real GDP Growth					
2	Is Asia recession-p					
3	Source: Internation					
4		1988	1989	1990	1991	
5	NICS	9.5	5.5	6.3		
6	Japan	5.6	5	5.3		
7	EC	3.9	3.5	3		
8						
9						

Data - Untitled-3

Title Set selected cells as... Display location of...

E8

Figure 18.2 *Imported data in the Data Manager.*

To see the data charted, click the **Chart View** at the top of the Toolbar. The bar chart, as shown in Figure 18.3, is displayed on the screen.

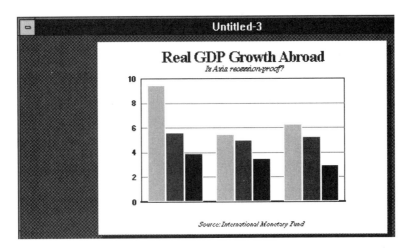

Figure 18.3 *Imported data charted as a bar chart.*

If you'd like to see both the Data Manager and the chart on the screen at the same time, select Tile Vertically from the Windows menu, and the Data Manager and chart are displayed side by side.

CHANGING A CHART'S APPEARANCE

Once the chart is displayed on the screen, you can change any element in the chart by selecting that menu element and accessing the Context Sensitive pop-up menu for that element. Either click on the Context Sensitive tool on the toolbar (right under the Pick tool), or click the right mouse button after you have selected the element.

CHANGING THE BAR THICKNESS

Let's start by changing the thickness of the bars on the bar chart. Select the element by clicking on any bar with the left mouse button. Then, click the right mouse button, and the Bar Thickness pop-up menu, displayed in Figure 18.4, is displayed.

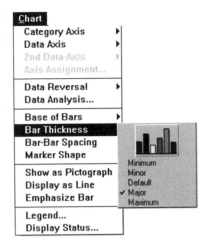

Figure 18.4 *The Bar Thickness pop-up menu.*

To see how really easy this is, select the bar, click on the right mouse button, and select **Minimum**. The chart is redrawn, as displayed in Figure 18.5.

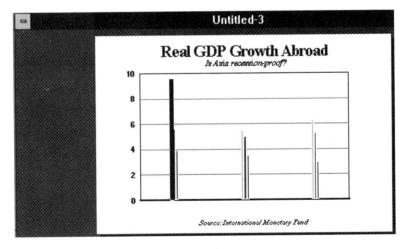

Figure 18.5 *The bar thickness set to Minimum.*

REVERSING THE DATA

You may want to see how the data looks if the data is reversed. In the bar chart we've been working with, the data for NICS appears first. To reverse the data, select **Data Reversal** from the Chart menu, and from the pop-up menu shown, select **Reverse Series**. The bar chart is now displayed with the EC data first, as shown in Figure 18.6.

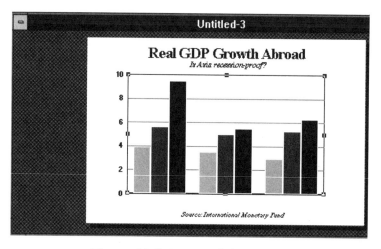

Figure 18.6 *A reversed data series.*

SCALE AND GRID

Often, the same data can look quite different depending on the scale it is displayed in. For example, using a different scale can eliminate more extreme numbers from a chart.

When CorelCHART draws a chart using the automatic scale range, it sets the scale to include the highest and lowest values represented in the data. In the example shown, 10 is the highest value along the vertical axis because the highest value in the data charted is 9.5, and 2 is the lowest value because 2.7 is the lowest value in the data. Let's look at a few examples to see how changing the scale can both alter a chart's appearance and change how the numbers appear relative to each other.

To change the scale on the Y (vertical) axis, click on any number along the axis, then click the right mouse button. From the pop-up menu shown, select **Scale Range** and the Scale Range dialog box, shown in Figure 18.7, is displayed.

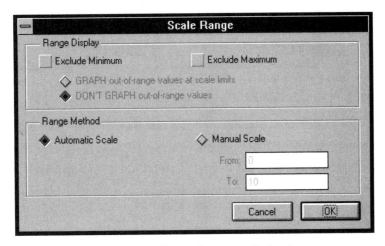

Figure 18.7 *The Scale Range dialog box.*

Click off **Automatic Scale** and click on **Manual Scale**. Enter 0 as the From value, and change the To value to 16. Click on **OK**, and the chart appears as displayed in Figure 18.8.

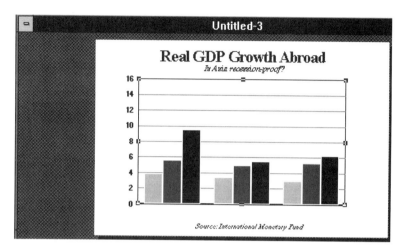

Figure 18.8 The chart redrawn with a vertical scale of 0 to 16.

By "flattening" the bars, the chart makes it look as though all of the regions are essentially the same, which is quite inaccurate. Let's experiment some more. Select the **Scale Range** dialog box again, but this time, enter 2 in the To box, but click on **Graph Out of Range Values at Scale Limits**. This has the effect of making all values above 8 appear equal, as displayed in Figure 18.9.

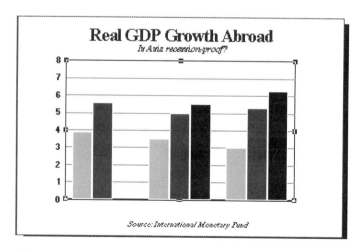

Figure 18.9 The chart redrawn with a vertical scale 0 to 8.

To put yet another slant on the same numbers, return to the Scale Range dialog box, and change From back to 2.

You can make your chart a little easier to read by adding grid marks. Click on any number along the axis and click the right mouse button. From the pop-up menu shown, select **Grid Lines**, and the Grid Lines dialog box, shown in Figure 18.10, is displayed.

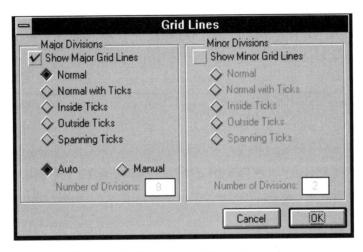

Figure 18.10 *The Grid Lines dialog box.*

From the Major Divisions option on the left side of the dialog box, check **Show Major Grid Lines**, then click on **Normal with Ticks**. At the bottom, click on **Auto** and enter 6 in the Number of Divisions box, since the numbers on your scale range from 2 to 8. Click on **OK**. The chart reappears with grid lines along the vertical axis, as displayed in Figure 18.11.

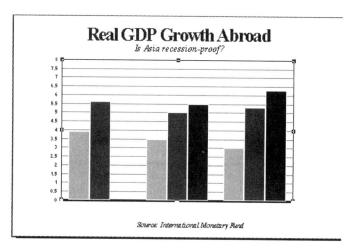

Figure 18.11 *The chart displayed with grid lines.*

CHOOSING ANOTHER CHART TYPE

CorelCHART makes it very easy for you to change chart types "on the fly," letting you experiment and see which type of chart best represents the data. To see how this data would look as a 3D riser chart, choose **3D Riser** from the Gallery menu. From the fly-out menu shown, choose **Bars**.

The chart reappears, as shown in Figure 18.12.

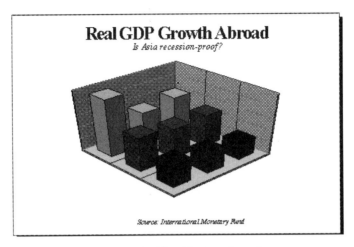

Figure 18.12 *The 3D riser bar chart.*

Just as we did with the bar chart, we can change the appearance of the 3D riser bar chart. Select any one of the bars and click the right mouse button. Click on **Data Reversal** and choose **Reverse Series**. The 3D Riser Bar chart is now displayed as shown in Figure 18.13.

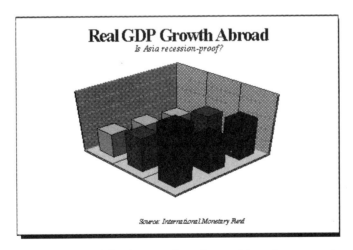

Figure 18.13 *The 3D riser bar chart with series reversed.*

On a 3D Riser chart, you can also change the viewing angles of the bars in the chart. From the Chart menu, select **Preset Viewing Angles**. From the pop-up menu shown, select one of the viewing angles (don't forget to check the preview box at the top of the pop-up menu to see how the view will actually appear). Figure 18.14 shows how your chart will look with the Column's Eye viewing angle selected.

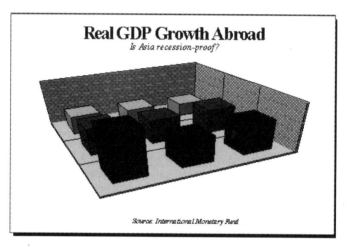

Figure 18.14 The 3D riser bar chart with the column's eye viewing angle.

The contents of the Chart menu vary with the type of chart you are currently working with.

Before we proceed to look at some different types of charts, note that although, so far, we've worked with Vertical Bar Charts, you can also display data horizontally, as shown in Figure 18.15.

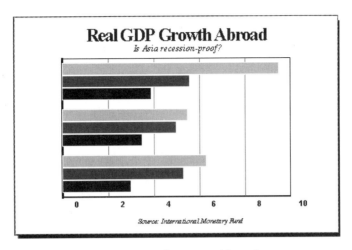

Figure 18.15 *A horizontal bar chart.*

ADDING FILLS

While we're looking at this chart, let's see how we can spruce it up a bit. Adding a fountain fill to enhance your chart works the same way that it does in CorelDRAW. Select the object you want and select the **Fountain Fill** button from the Fill tool fly-out menu. The Fountain Fill dialog box, shown in Figure 18.16 is displayed.

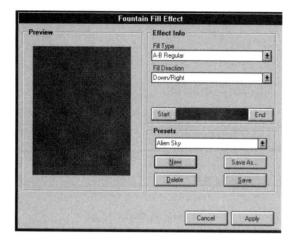

Figure 18.16 *The Fountain Fill dialog box.*

Select the fill and color you want for the selected element and click on
OK. The fountain fill is applied to your chart, as shown in figure 18.17.

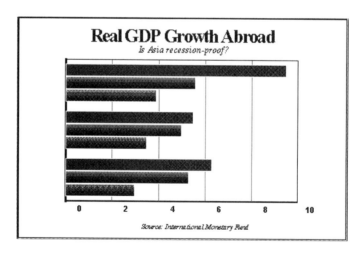

Figure 18.17 *A fountain fill applied to bar a chart.*

DISPLAYING A CHART ON THE SCREEN

While you are working with your chart, it's a good idea to make the view of the chart as large as possible, and to display all of the chart elements that fit on the screen. However, you may wish to display or hide certain elements to make your chart easier to understand. To help you display or hide elements, select **Display Status** from the Chart menu. The Display Status dialog box, pictured in Figure 18.18, is displayed.

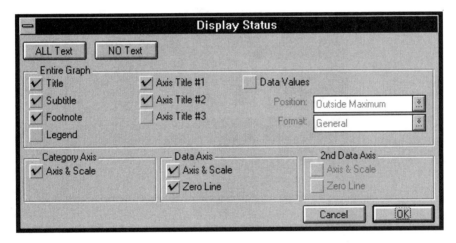

Figure 18.18 *The Display Status dialog box.*

Click on the checkboxes for the elements you want to show and click off the checkboxes for the elements that you want to hide. Then click on **OK** and look at the revised view of your chart.

You can also enlarge the entire view of the chart on the screen by resizing the Window.

USING TEXT AND GRAPHICS

Change the look of your chart by changing the fonts for any text element in your chart. Click on the text you want to change. From the Text Ribbon at the top of the screen, select the font you want from the list box in the left corner. Figure 18.19 shows the font changed to Arial in the chart title.

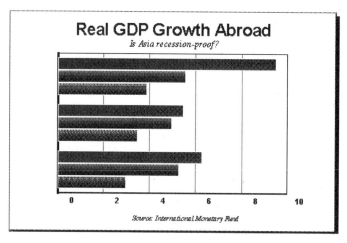

Figure 18.19 *The chart title shown in the Arial font.*

From the Text Ribbon you can amend the style as well as the font, using the style icons.

You can also change the point size or justification from the Text Ribbon.

To further explain the data shown in your chart, add an annotation anywhere on the chart. Select the text tool, then drag a text frame over the area of the chart where you want to place the annotation. Once the frame is placed, type in your text. Figure 18.20 shows annotation placed in an empty spot on the chart.

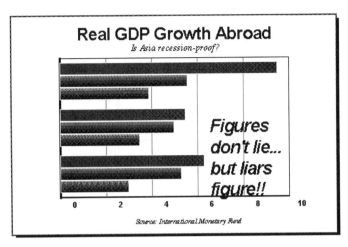

Figure 18.20 *The chart with annotation.*

ADDING A GRAPHIC

You can include a graphic on your chart to give it some pictorial interest. You can use one of the symbols in your True Type font set, or you can import a graphic from CorelDRAW. Figure 18.21 shows a graphic added to a chart.

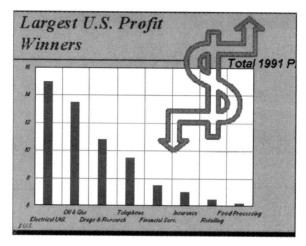

Figure 18.21 *A graphic added to a bar chart.*

SELECTING THE BEST CHART TYPE

As you can see, CorelCHART offers a variety of chart types. Experiment with any type you like, but certain types of data are best represented by one or more specific types of charts.

BAR CHARTS

Use *vertical bar charts* to show how data changes over time, for example, comparing the information for several years. A variation on the bar chart is the *stacked bar*, which can show how different parts contributed to a whole. For example, if a bar chart showed the performance of a company over several years, a stacked bar chart can show how much profit each division of the company generated in each of the years displayed.

Several variations on the vertical bar chart represent the same information in a different way.

You can also enliven a bar chart by creating a pictograph. Select one of the bars, then, from the Chart menu, choose **Show as Pictograph**. From the Fill fly-out menu, select the **Vectors tool** (the double-headed arrow), then choose one of the available vector patterns. Figure 18.23 shows a bar chart illustration as a pictograph.

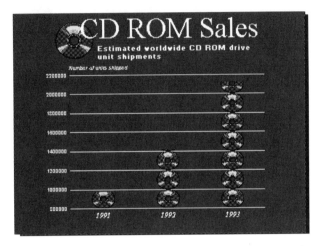

Figure 18.23 *A bar chart illustrated as a pictograph.*

Horizontal bar charts, are good for representing variations in values within a specific time frame.

LINE CHARTS

Now let's take a look at another of the major chart types, the *line chart*. This type of chart works better if your values represent changes in a small group of values over a long period of time. Figure 18.24 through Figure 18.26 shows a line chart, a 3D ribbon chart, and a vertical area chart.

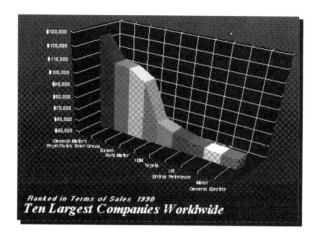

Figure 18.24 *A line chart.*

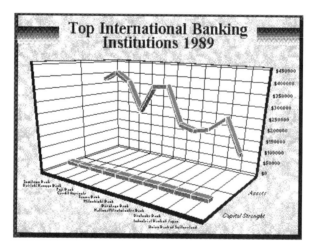

Figure 18.25 *A 3D ribbon chart.*

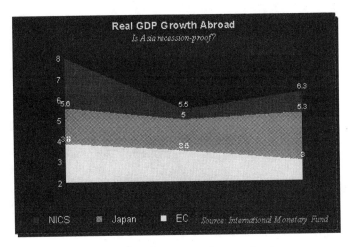

Figure 18.26 *A vertical area chart.*

PIE CHARTS

Pie charts are most effective if you wish to show how different parts contribute to a whole (in other words, to show percentages). Figure 18.27 shows a ring pie chart.

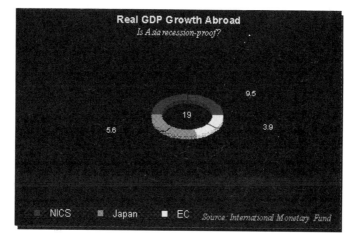

Figure 18.27 *A ring pie chart.*

To represent the same type of data over a period of time, use multiple pie charts, as shown in Figure 18.28.

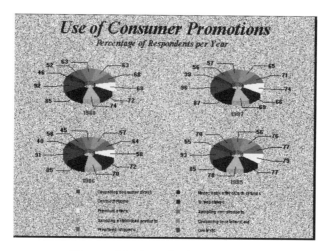

Figure 18.28 *Multiple pie charts.*

The best way to decide which type of chart to use is to begin with some of these basic guidelines, then experiment. Because CorelCHART makes it so easy to redraw a chart with any type from its Gallery, you can preview what each selection will look like and you can make changes at any time.

SUMMARY

In this chapter, you've learned how to use the basics of CorelCHART to chart any information and visually present it in the best way possible. To help you design and display your chart, you've learned how to:

▼ Begin a chart, including importing data and selecting a chart type.

▼ Change the appearance of any chart elements.

▼ Modify the way data is represented by changing the values on the horizontal or vertical axis.

▼ Rearrange graph elements.

▼ Add color and fill.

▼ Use text and graphics.

▼ Select the best chart type for the job.

CREATING A CORELSHOW PRESENTATION

CorelSHOW lets you put together objects from a variety of applications and create a presentation consisting of multiple pages or slides.

This chapter covers:

▼ Getting started.
▼ The presentation screen.
▼ Creating a slide show.

Input for CorelSHOW can come from CorelDRAW, CorelCHART, or any other Object Linking and Embedding (OLE) application. The output you create can be in the form of an animated screen show, slides, overheads, or series of panels that you can later print. If you're creating an on-screen presentation, you can be a real film maker, deciding how long each image remains on the screen and using transition effects to make a more professional move from one view to the next.

For the sake of this discussion, we will call each page or view of a presentation a *slide*.

NOTE

CorelSHOW is an *OLE assembler program*. This means that it can link or embed an object from CorelDRAW, CorelCHART, or any other server application. When you embed an object you actually insert information from the source file (in this instance, the CorelDRAW or other file) into the destination document in another application (such as CorelSHOW). If you link the object, you do not insert the file information, but only the link to the object's location. When linked or embedded objects are edited, their source application is launched to provided the necessary tools. To use OLE to link and embed objects, *you must be running under Windows 3.1.*

GETTING STARTED

First let's define a few terms. A *background* is exactly what it implies—it is the backdrop against which a slide is viewed. If you've ever been to a photographer's studio, think of it as the drape that was placed behind you to give a particular effect to your portrait.

There are three ways of viewing or editing a presentation.

1. **Background View** edits the background in each slide in the background

2. **Slide View** views and edits individual slides. CorelSHOW allows multiple document viewing, which lets you to open several files at one time, and to move or copy information from one file to another.

3. **Slide Sorter View** views the entire presentation.

THE PRESENTATION SCREEN

The CorelSHOW screen has several elements, as shown in Figure 19.1.

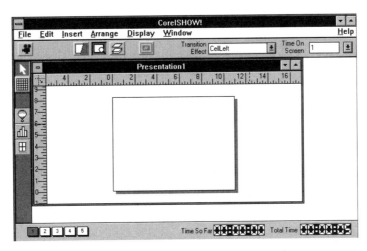

Figure 19.1 *The CorelSHOW screen.*

THE CORELSHOW MENU

The top line of the screen includes the name of the application, CorelSHOW. The following line is the menu bar, which lists the following items:

▼ **File** opens, saves, closes, and prints files, and runs a screen show.

▼ **Edit** cuts, copies, and pastes operations, or undoes a previous command.

▼ **Insert** inserts, embeds, or links an object or file into a slide show.

▼ **Arrange** organizes objects on top of each other.

▼ **Display** places rulers and guidelines to help you arrange the presentation.

▼ **Window** manages the screen view.

▼ **Help** accesses CorelSHOW interactive help.

THE TOOLBAR

The Toolbar along the left edge of the screen shows the following tools:

▼ **Pick** selects, moves, or resizes objects.

▼ **Background Library** select backgrounds for a slide show.

▼ **OLE to CorelDRAW** provides a gateway to CorelDRAW applications.

▼ **OLE to CorelCHART** provides a gateway to CorelCHART applications.

▼ **OLE to Other Applications** Provides a fly-out menu to access any other OLE applications.

VIEWING MODE BUTTONS

Under the Menu bar are three buttons that represent the three viewing modes.

1. **Background View** views and edits the background that you will use for each slide in the show. To let you work directly on the background, the slide shows disappears. While you are working in Background View, you can use the tools in the Toolbar to access objects from other applications.

2. **Slide View** lets you view and edit the individual slides on which you are working while you assemble the slides in your show. When you're working in Slide View, you can use the tools in the Toolbar to access objects from other applications.

3. **Slide Sorter View** gives you a miniaturized view of each slide in the show. If all of your slides do not fit on the screen, use the vertical scroll bars to page through the slides. Use the Slide Sorter View to arrange the slides in your show by dragging the slides around the window to a new location, or you can access the Cut, Copy, and Paste options from the Edit menu. If you move one slide while you're working in this mode, all of the others automatically move to accommodate the change.

   From the Slide Sorter View, use the Numbering Tool to number the slides in the show. By clicking, in succession, on each slide in the show you can rearrange the slides without physically moving them around. When you've numbered all of the slides, click on the **Numbering Tool** again, and the slides are rearranged on the screen.

TRANSITION EFFECTS

Click on **Transition Effects** to see the transition effects list, which lets you make transitions between each slide. The transition effects list is shown below:

▼ HorizBlind

▼ HorizBlindDissolve

▼ VertBlind

- ▼ VertBlinDissolve
- ▼ WipeDown
- ▼ WipeLeft
- ▼ WipeRight
- ▼ Wipeup
- ▼ ZoomIn
- ▼ ZoomOnShow
- ▼ ZoomInFast
- ▼ ZoomInDissolve
- ▼ ZoomOut
- ▼ ZoomOutShow
- ▼ ZoomOutFast
- ▼ ZoomOutDissolve
- ▼ Animation

TIME ON SCREEN

Use Time on Screen to specify the amount of time the selected slide remains on the screen.

PAGE ICONS

In the bottom-left corner of the screen are the icons of all of the slides in the current presentation. The slide on which you are currently working is grayed. Use the page icons to move directly to the slide on which you want to work.

SHOW CLOCKS

In the bottom-right corner of the screen you'll see Show Clocks, which displays the total running time of the slide show, and the time that has elapsed so far.

CREATING A SLIDE SHOW

To illustrate how to create a slide show presentation, use the sample show included with CorelSHOW. When you open the application, you'll see a Welcome screen.

If you'd like to see what we'll be trying to accomplish, select **Open an Existing Presentation**, and choose IFONLY.SHW from the File Name list shown. Click on **OK** to return to the main screen. Then, select **Run Screen Show** from the File menu, and sit back and enjoy the show.

1. Select **Start a New Presentation**. Change the number of slides to 5.
2. Click on **Page Setup**.
3. From the Page Setup dialog box, choose **Screen** and then click on **OK**.
4. When you return to the Welcome screen, click on **OK** to return to the main screen.

CHOOSING THE BACKGROUND

Let's begin assembling the slide show by choosing the background.

1. Click on the **Background View** button at the top of the screen, and then click on the **Background Library** button at the left of the screen.

2. From the Select Background dialog shown in Figure 19.2, make sure that the List Files of Type box is set to *.SHB.

3. From the subdirectory Samples in the SHOW directory, select IFONLY.SHB, then click on **Done**. Figure 19.3 graphically shows the backgrounds that are available in the library.

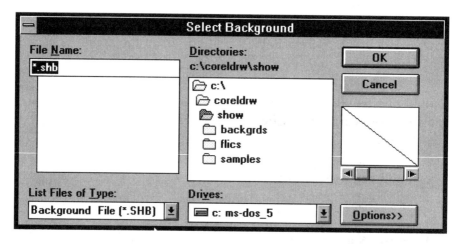

Figure 19.2 *The Select Background dialog box.*

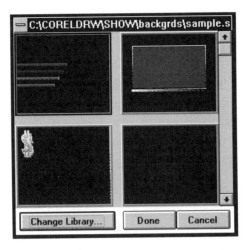

Figure 19.3 *Available backgrounds.*

SELECTING THE SLIDES

The slides we want to use in our presentation are in CorelDRAW and CorelCHART. We will also use an animation file to add excitement to our presentation.

LINKING TO A CORELDRAW FILE

Because our first slide is in CorelDRAW, go to that application and create a link to the drawing we need.

1. Minimize CorelSHOW by clicking on the Minimize button.
2. Start CorelDRAW by double-clicking on its icon in the Program Manager group.
3. Select **Open** from the File menu.
4. In the Open Drawing dialog box, make sure that your directory is set to D:\CORELDRW.SAMPLES and select IFONLY2.CDR.

5. Click on **OK** to return to the CorelDRAW screen.

6. Make sure that all of your objects are selected, then select **Copy** from the Edit menu. The object is placed on the Windows Clipboard.

7. Now that we've chosen the slide, we'll want to return to CorelSHOW. Minimize CorelDRAW, and maximize the CorelSHOW icon that you see at the bottom of your screen.

8. From the Edit menu, select **Paste Special**.

9. From the Paste Special dialog box shown in Figure 19.4, select **Type of Object** from the list on the left side of the box, then click on **Paste Link**.

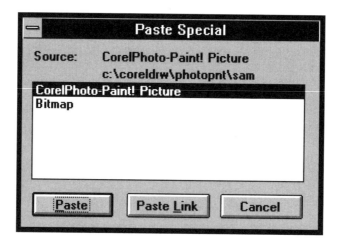

Figure 19.4 *The Paste Special dialog box.*

10. Your object now appears on the CorelSHOW screen with handles around it, as shown in Figure 19.5.

Figure 19.5 *The object pasted into CorelSHOW.*

11. Much as you did with CorelDRAW, you can move the object around the "slide," or resize it to fit the slide. For this slide show, let's center the object on the slide.

If you want to edit the object, for example, if you'd like to change the lettering to white like you saw in the sample show, double-click on the object. This returns you to CorelDRAW, where you can select the lettering and choose white from the palette. When you're done, select **Copy** from the Edit menu, close CorelDRAW, and return to CorelSHOW.

LINKING A CHART FROM CORELCHART

Next, let's embed text from CorelDRAW and a chart from CorelCHART.

1. Select the page icon for the second slide from the bottom of the screen.

2. Select **File** from the Insert menu. The Insert File dialog box, shown in Figure 19.6, is displayed.

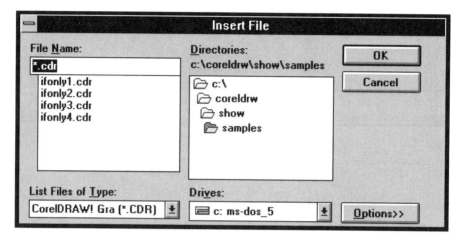

Figure 19.6 *The Insert File dialog box.*

3. Click on the **Options** button, then click on the radio buttons **Link to File** and **Add to Current Page.**

4. Select IFONLY3.CDR from the file name list and click on **OK**. The object is displayed on your second slide. Use the Pick tool to move or resize the object so that it is centered in the second slide.

5. To add the chart to the slide show, select **File** from the Insert menu, click on **Options**, then click on the radio buttons **Link to File** and **Add to Current Page**.

6. This time, choose IFONLY4.CCH from the file name list and click on **OK** Use the Pick tool to move or resize the chart.

7. The third slide consists of a CorelDRAW text file, so follow the procedure we just learned. Select **File** from the Insert menu, click on **Options** and choose **Link to File** and **Add to Current Page,** and select IFONLY4.CDR.

ANIMATION

Add some animation to complete the group of slides for our show. Select the page icon for the fourth slide, then choose **Animation** from the Insert menu. The Insert Animation dialog box is displayed. Click on the file name IFONLY5.FLI and the file opens in full-screen mode.

THE SLIDE SORTER

If you'd like to rearrange the slides, click on the **Slide Sorter** icon (the third icon under the menu bar). Click on the fourth slide (the animation that we just added) and drag it between the second and third slide. Release the mouse button, and the fourth slide is now the third (and the third slide is now fourth).

SAVING A SLIDE SHOW

Save the entire slide show. Select **Save As** from the File menu. In the Save Presentation As dialog box, shown in Figure 19.7, name the new file IFONLY1.SHW (to distinguish it from the sample slide show you saw earlier). You can also add keywords or notes to the file to jog your memory when you go to retrieve it later.

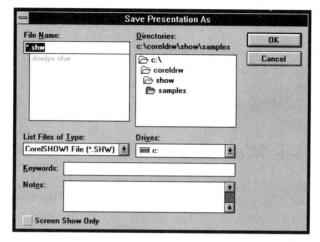

Figure 19.7 *The Save Presentation As dialog box.*

VIEWING A SLIDE SHOW

To see how your slide show turned out, select **Run Screen Show** from the File menu. Because you've already saved it, feel free to make any changes you like, in color, transitional effects, or even the contents of the slides themselves. Because these are OLE objects, you can always go back to the source application and edit them in whatever way is needed.

SUMMARY

In this chapter you've learned how to use the CorelSHOW application to assemble objects from a variety of applications and arrange them into a slide show (or screen presentation). You've seen how to use CorelSHOW to assemble various elements in a slide show, including:

▼ Viewing the CorelSHOW Screen, incorporating the CorelSHOW Toolbar, and the three viewing modes.

▼ Including Transition Effects in the slide show.

▼ Using an OLE assembler program to link or embed an object from another application.

▼ Creating the background for the slide show.

▼ Consolidating graphics, text, charts, and animation into a slide show presentation.

▼ Saving the slide show.

▼ Viewing the slide show

INDEX